They lived in Sharrow and Nether Edge

A miscellany by the Nether Edge Neighbourhood Group
Local History Section

This book is gratefully dedicated to
MARY WALTON
The first historian of Sharrow and Nether Edge

CONTENTS

The Origins of Sharrow and Nether Edge	Giles Robinson	3
The Reverend Alexander MacKenzie	Joan Flett	6
The Newboulds of Sharrow Bank	Joan Flett	8
The Last Remains of Upper Edge		11
The Wilsons and the Snuff Mill	Susan Cleary	12
Public Service and Private Profit	Shirley Meek	15
George Wostenholm	Giles Robinson, with Lois Everson and Edward Oldfield	21
John Rodgers	Giles Robinson	25
Thomas Steade	Giles Robinson	26
The Boot Family	Shirley Meek and Joyce Jenkinson	27
Sir John Brown at Shirle Hill	Joan Flett	30
Thomas Jessop	Irene Clegg	32
The Smiths	Giles Robinson	33
James Montgomery	Malcolm Weston	36
Charles Peace	Malcolm Weston	37
John Cole of Prior Bank	Joan Flett	38
They Built Nether Edge	Giles Robinson	40
The Nether Edge Bowling Club	Janet Hartley	45
Old Houses at the top of Glen Road	Janet Hartley	47
The Brinkcliffe Tower Estate	Audrey Stanton	50
My First School	Ruby McDonald	52
The Shops of Nether Edge	Mrs Jackson and Mrs Jarman	53
The Way It Was . . .	Mrs Jackson and others	54
The Lantern Theatre	Mary Walton and Ruby McDonald	55
Changes at Sharrow Vale	Margaret Andrews	57
Tom Whittaker	Jackie Hamilton	58
Laurence Mullins	Joan Oldfield and Betty and Harold Howe	59
Leslie Perkins de Abrew	Joan Oldfield	60
First School Days	Jimmi Eldridge	61
Wilf Green	Malcolm Weston	62
Memories of Nether Edge in the 1940 Blitz	Shirley Meek	64
Acknowledgements		71
References		72

© Nether Edge Local History Group 1988

ISBN: 1-901587-10-X

Front Cover: A croquet party in the grounds of Kenwood House in the 1870s.

Beneath the districts of Sharrow and Nether Edge lie the sandstones of the Coal Measures, formed over 280 million years ago and worn by wind, rain and the effects of the Ice Age into the landscape of today. The rocks yield many fossils of the plants which were growing here all those millions of years ago. I found a fine horsetail plant fossil this year, thrown up by the excavations for the Methodist old people's homes on Psalter Lane, and as a child I dug up a bit of fossil tree root in our family back garden on Herbert Road.

The stones of our area have been extensively quarried along Brincliffe Edge since at least the fifteenth century. The rock is, at its best, a beautiful fine grained sandstone, which does however have a tendency to split or flake. It was used mainly for items such as window sills, steps and gateposts, though near the quarries it was used as a general building stone. Brincliffe Edge stone was also quarried for grindstones which, having a fine grain, were ideal for finishing work in the town and valley grinding shops. The best relic of the quarrying days is the rock left behind on Psalter Lane when the Salt Box cottages were demolished. It is all that is left of the hillside which has been worked away around it. This strange relic looks very beautiful with the sunset light upon it, when it has the air of an ancient monument.

We will never know when man first visited the Sharrow and Nether Edge area, but the prehistoric hunter-gatherers must have surely crossed through the great woodlands which then covered the district. Their camp sites have been located all around the Sheffield area, for example at Totley, Treeton, Wincobank and Ringinglow. Sadly, the evidence for early history in much of Sheffield and its suburbs has been obscured by continuous development, so we must turn to Anglo Saxon and early Norman times to begin the story of Sharrow and Nether Edge.

The earliest settlements in the district were Little Sheffield and Heeley. In late Anglo Saxon times they both lay in the lands of Hallamshire, a great Saxon estate which was divided up into districts such as Ecclesfield, Bradfield, and Ecclesall. Hallamshire gets its name from Hallam, which was a village near Lodge Moor on the old Roman road from the fort at Templeborough near Rotherham to the fort at Brough near Castleton. Hallam lost its importance as Sheffield became the district's centre in Norman times.

The origins of Sharrow and Nether Edge

◆ Giles Robinson

Little Sheffield and Sheffield almost certainly stand in the same relationship as hundreds of other villages with paired names such as Great and Little Driffield, or North and South Anston. One village of the pair would develop out of the other, perhaps by a shift in the population or, as happened in the case of the Sheffields, by the setting up of a church, a market or a castle at one village to the detriment of the other.

If the name Sheffield means field or cleared land by the Sheaf we can look at the two Sheffields with new interest. Sheffield proper had its own town fields on the side of town away from the river Sheaf. It was also separated from this river by a fairly steep valley side (the drop between Arundel Gate and Pond Street) and by a swampy, flood-prone area which was later transformed into fish ponds and a mill dam giving rise to the name Pond Street. Little Sheffield stood where London Road now joins St Mary's Gate, and before the huge Sheffield Park was constructed its town fields stretched straight down to the Sheaf. This makes it possible that Little Sheffield is the true Sheaf Field. It is also probable that the Saxons used the place name 'field' to denote land already

Machon Bank Farm, pictured in the 19th century, stood on the same site as it had done in medieval times.

Looking down from Brincliffe Edge to where Archer Lane joins Bannerdale Road about 1900, this view shows the change from farmland to suburbia has begun.

cleared by the time they came here, which may point to the existence of a Romano-British settlement at Sheffield.

From early medieval times until late in the thirteenth century many new farms were made all over England as the population grew. Plenty of land was available for the creation of these new settlements and for the enlargement of old ones. This was probably the time when most of the important farms in the Sharrow and Nether Edge district were set up, some perhaps by families from Little Sheffield and Heeley. Once created, the pattern of farms continued in existence largely unchanged, except for small additions and divisions, until the suburbs swept over the area in the nineteenth century.

The farm of Priory Grange, which stood near the corner of Priory Road and Sharrow Lane, is an example of an early medieval establishment. It was set up on behalf of Worksop Priory in the twelfth or thirteenth century. In later days it was called Stocks Farm, and if the area of Stocks Farm revealed by a map of about 1800 is all land cleared for the Grange then it accounts for a large part of our district. However, its large size is not typical of the usual scale of farm clearances.

The lands belonging to the hamlet of Machon Bank, which once stood where Machon Bank Road meets Joshua and Emily Roads, were also early medieval clearances. Machon Bank was originally Hawslin Bank, taking its name from the Hawslin family of Little Sheffield who were perhaps responsible for turning this land into farmland. Cherry Tree Farm, which stood opposite the Union Hotel on Cherry Tree Road, may have been a later sub-division of Machon Bank's original land. The hamlet of Machon Bank was demolished to make way for terraced housing about 1903 and Cherry Tree Farm was also pulled down in 1906 so that Meadow Bank Avenue could be built.

Country residences, as opposed to farm houses, started to appear in the eighteenth century. In 1800 only a few existed, some of which were built on older sites. Sharrow Head House, for example, was built on to a seventeenth century house; The Edge, on Ladysmith Avenue, incorporated part of a seventeenth century building including a mullioned window on an inside wall (removed during recent renovation); and

Mount Pleasant, on Sharrow Lane, was built on the site of an older house. Two late eighteenth century residences which were built on new sites were Brightfield House, built in 1790 at the bottom of Sharrow Lane, and Violet Bank, a square Georgian house built in 1794 which stood where Raven Road is today.

Between 1800 and 1850 more country residences or villas came into existence. Several of these, such as Kenwood, Sharrow Bank, Audrey Cottage and Abbeydale House, are mentioned in other articles in this book. Gatefield House (which still stands between Abbeydale Road and Sandford Grove Road) was built about 1835, and both Osborne House, on the corner of Brincliffe Crescent and Kingfield Road and Brincliffe Cottage, on the corner of Osborne Road and Psalter Lane, were built about 1840.

By 1850 we are on the verge of large scale suburban development. Already the first outposts of what George Orwell called 'villa civilisation' had been built, and within a few more years the other important elements of the suburb had been laid out, around which all subsequent development was to take place. These were the Kenwood Park development, the Nether Edge estate, Brincliffe Towers and Chippinghouse. The first new streets, laid out ready for houses to be built, were also in existence by 1850. These were Osborne Road, Brincliffe Crescent and Kingfield Road, of about 1842, and Union Road, of about 1845. The property developments which shaped the suburb of Sharrow and Nether Edge now followed. The large scale developments of Wostenholm, Steade and the Newbould family are all covered later in this book, together with some examples of smaller undertakings by speculative builders and private individuals.

An exception to the general pattern of suburban development in the area was the building up of the Nether Edge estate on the lands of the Nether Edge farm. The farmhouse still stands as the Brincliffe Oaks Hotel. Although it no longer has its outbuildings, which in 1851 included a stable, coach houses, brew house and barn, it still has part of its late seventeenth century structure. In the wall facing Oakhill Road the original mullioned windows can still be seen, although the other side was rebuilt in the nineteenth century and there have been more recent additions.

In February 1853 the Nether Edge estate was purchased by the Reform Freehold Building Society for £7,000. This was a and society', whose trustees would purchase land and divide up into building plots. The members of the society could buy these plots, paying by instalments instead of having to find a large lump sum. This enabled less well-off artisans to get their own homes, and at the same time to become eligible for the vote.

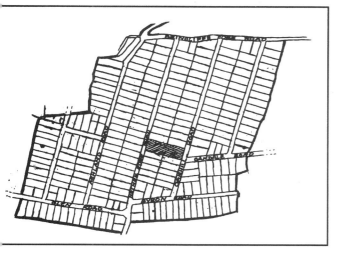

Nether Edge Estate, as planned by Samuel Furness Holmes in 1853. The shaded rectangle shows Nether Edge Farm.

The Reform Freehold Building Society already had estates at Crookes and Heeley. Samuel Furness Holmes, surveyor and architect, was appointed to survey and lay out the land but 'at his recommendation it has been thought best not to commence operations until the crops of the year shall have been reaped'.

The plan for division was ready by December 1853 and the next year the work of constructing 'carriage roads, footpaths, common sewers, pumps and other works' was done. The plan of the estate can be seen in the map. The Montgomery Land Society took over the estate in 1861, and under this organisation the work of selling plots for building was continued until 1883 when the society was closed.

The streets being laid out all over the new suburb were filled with houses in two different ways. Firstly, by private individuals who bought land and had their own homes built for them, and secondly by property sepculators of one sort or another.

Speculative building is the putting up of houses to sell or to rent, in anticipation of public demand. As the nineteenth century went on suburban development increasingly took place in this way. Most of the speculation was done by those who were builders by trade, but people from every kind of background tried their hand at this method of making money. Cutlery manufacturers, steel makers, grocers, solicitors; anyone might become involved, even if only to the extent of one or two houses.

Profit was the main motive for engaging in property development, but not always the only one. Some developers, for example George Wostenholm, were anxious to control the character of their neighbourhood. The Brincliffe Estates Company Ltd, set up in 1898 to try and develop parts of Kingfield Road and Brincliffe Crescent, was started by the people living close by who had in forming their plans 'been mainly influenced by the desire to preserve the property from becoming a disfigurement to the neighbourhood by the erection of inferior houses'. Land deals frequently made provisions to ensure a certain quality of house, either by setting a minimum limit on their cost or by specifying the building materials to be used.

Nevertheless the building of Sharrow and Nether Edge was in the main carried out to make money rather than with the specific object of creating a beautiful suburb. We are fortunate that many individuals and speculative builders did set high standards and so produced the numerous fine buildings which still remain today.

The select and leafy Kenwood Estate as George Wostenholm must have envisaged it.

Kenwood Park Rd   JWM.

The Reverend Alexander MacKenzie

◆ Joan Flett

Chance brought Alexander MacKenzie to Sheffield far from his family roots in distant Perthshire. He became firstly the Curate of the Parish Church and, secondly, the Vicar of St Paul's Church which stood on the site of the Peace Gardens until its demolition in 1938.

Alexander was born in 1755, the elder son of Colin MacKenzie, at the family estate of Finegand, near Kirkmichael, in Glen Shee. His younger brother, Patrick, was born in 1758. He was a Gaelic speaker and writer and was educated at St Andrew's University. He then entered the Church and apparently received an episcopal ordination which later enabled him to hold an English incumbency.

After various family tragedies the two brothers came under the patronage of the Duke of Atholl and in 1778, after his ordination, Alexander became a Chaplain in the Atholl Highlanders in which his brother also served as an Ensign. The Regiment served mainly in Ireland and after it was disbanded in 1783 Alexander went to India where he was Chaplain to the Earl of Eglintoun and Patrick joined the 1st Royals Regiment.

When he returned home from India in 1787 Alexander travelled with Admiral Gell. The Admiral was related by marriage to various local families and, in particular, to the Reverend James Wilkinson, Vicar of Sheffield Parish Church, to whom he introduced Alexander. The Vicar took an immediate liking to him and appointed him his Curate. As the Reverend Wilkinson had his own residence at Broomhall, Alexander lived at the Vicarage. In 1788 he married Margaret Smith, daughter of Susan and Thomas Smith of Sheffield. Susan was one of the Battie family of Sharrow Head House (see 'The Newboulds of Sharrow Bank') and, through her mother Margaret, inherited that estate. The following year Alexander was appointed Vicar of St Paul's Church where he remained for the next twenty-eight years and he resided at Sharrow Head House.

The Rev. Alexander MacKenzie.

Alexander was the fourth incumbent of St Paul's. The Church had been founded largely at the instigation of Robert Downes, a goldsmith, who gave £1,000 towards the building and £30 a year towards the support of the minister. The rest of the stipend of the ministers and the curates was derived from the letting of seats and pews in the Church. The seats were let at not less than an average of 4s. each a year and an amount of not less than £30 was paid to the minister and the remainder to the curate. Seats and pews were often bequeathed in wills and sometimes sold at public auctions. The foundation stone of St Paul's had been laid in 1720 but, due to a disagreement over the patronage, the Church was not consecrated until 1740. When St Paul's was built there were few houses between the Parish Church and the bottom of The Moor and the two Churches served a population of 10,000. However, with the growing expansion of industry in the Town St Paul's quickly became a fashionable church and many well-known families were members of its large congregation. They included Thomas Bolsover, the discoverer of Sheffield Plate, and Samuel Roberts, the 'Paupers' Advocate' who wrote such vitriolic pamphlets about the Poor Law Amendment Act and about the Workhouse at Nether Edge. Other members of the congregation included the Jessops, the Mappins and Dr Younge, the founder of The Royal Infirmary and its Medical Officer for forty-one years. Dr Younge lived at Sharrow Grange on Sharrow Lane and one visitor to the Town, in 1798, referred to Dr Younge's 'country house'.

Alexander appears to have been very striking physically. He was 6ft 4in tall and his hair had been grey since he was twenty years old. Joseph Hunter, the historian records, 'I well remember his tall majestic figure, and a certain air about him which indicated a consciousness of power'. He was obviously a vigorous, sophisticated man who was popular with his fashionable congregation. He revived choral music in the Church after a lapse of ten years and great concerts were held which attracted large audiences. He was President of the 'Pitt Club' formed about 1810 'to commemorate annually the virtues and distinguished talents of so illustrious a statesman as the late Rt Hon William Pitt'. The Club held 'very convivial' gatherings! He attended the Assembly Rooms in Norfolk Street where his mother-in-law had, at one time, been 'Queen of the Assembly' and, in spite of criticism, was apt to take part in the dancing. This would probably have seemed a perfectly natural activity to him.

St Paul's Church, formerly on Pinstone Street.

From at least the early part of the 18th century up until well into the 20th century the majority of Scottish children learned to dance. They either attended classes in the nearest town or, in the countryside, attended classes when the itinerent dancing master came round and held his session of ten or twelve classes. At those classes the children were taught their manners and the etiquette of the polite ballroom together with the current ballroom dances of the day and the popular Scottish solo dances. The classes were regarded as part of the social education of children and Alexander would almost certainly have attended such classes in his childhood. On a more serious side he was a member of the first Committee of the General Infirmary and Chaplain of the Sheffield Regiment of Volunteer Infantry. This regiment was disbanded in 1802 but, with the threat of invasion during the Napoleonic War, it was raised again 1803. It is recorded that, in 1808, there was a 'collection at St Paul's for the British prisoners in France, after a sermon by the Rev. A MacKenzie . . .'. It totalled £60 11s. 0d.

Alexander and his wife had several children who died young and one daughter, Margaret, who lived to be twenty-nine years old. His wife died in 1793 shortly after the birth of a son and Alexander took for his second wife Sarah, daughter of Joseph Wilson of the Snuff Mill. They had one daughter, Mary Ann, and her story is told in 'The Newboulds of Sharrow Bank'. Alexander and Sarah remained at Sharrow Head House and the old MacKenzie Walk and MacKenzie Street commemorate him as does The Stag public house. There had been a dilapidated hostelry at the top of Cemetery Road serving travellers on the turnpike from Sheffield to Chapel-en-le-Frith. Alexander arranged for this to be pulled down and had a new house built further along the present Psalter Lane. It was named The Stag's Head after the emblem on the family crest of the MacKenzie family.

On the death of his father Alexander inherited the family estate at Finegand. He employed a cousin, the Reverend Alexander Stewart, as his factor and administered the estate with great care. He was before his time in some of his ideas, one of which was to experiment with the planting of larch trees in the area. Whisky was also one of the products of the estate. The estate was eventually to be inherited by Mary Ann and then by her eldest son by her marriage to William Smith, a lawyer and attorney, of Barnes Hall, Grenoside.

Towards the end of his life Alexander suffered illness and pain from stones in his bladder. In an attempt to gain relief he travelled to London for a lithotomy operation. In order to avoid the jostling and jolting of a journey by road he was transported all the way on a canal boat lying in a hammock, a journey which took three days. He was operated on by an eminent surgeon and the operation was successful. However, he was then sixty-two years old, illness had taken its toll, his general health declined and he died on 30th November 1816, whilst still in London. His body was returned to Sheffield for burial in his own Church where he was joined only three years later by his daughter, Margaret, and a year after that by his brother, Patrick. Patrick had had a distinguished career in the army. He was Colonel of his Regiment in 1813 and, after forty-two years in the army, a Major General and a Colonel of the 3rd Veteran Royal Battalion. In spite of his service all over the world the two brothers had remained close friends and Patrick spent all his leaves with Alexander in Sheffield.

St Paul's Churchyard was destined not to be the final resting place of Alexander and his family. With the increasing commercialism of the Town centre the population began to move out to the growing suburbs leaving several churches less than viable. In 1933 a bill was passed in Parliament to allow seven Sheffield churches, including St Paul's, to be demolished. The Church was finally pulled down in 1938 and, at that time, 5,000 bodies had to be disinterred and buried elsewhere. Relatives of the dead were contacted where possible and some were able to make private arrangements for disposal. Alexander's descendent, Colonel William MacKenzie Smith of Barnes Hall, Grenoside, had married Lady Mabel Florence Harriet Wentworth Fitzwilliam, sister of the seventh Earl Fitzwilliam, and he had inherited the MacKenzie family estate in Perthshire. He and his wife arranged for the bodies to be cremated and the ashes interred in a crypt of the present Sheffield Cathedral.

General Patrick MacKenzie.

The Newboulds of Sharrow Bank

◆ Joan Flett

Sharrow Bank, about 1937.

When Miss Elizabeth Newbould died in Leamington Spa on the 27th April 1909, aged eighty-seven, she left monetary bequests to her sister-in-law and to various Sheffield organisations — £50 to The Royal Infirmary, £50 to The Royal Hospital and £50 to the Sheffield Girls' Charity School, Mount Pleasant — but the residue of her estate she left to her nephews and nieces. That estate was extensive. Locally it comprised virtually all of the area known from at least 1615, when it was sold by the Jessop family, as Cherry Tree Hill. It was bounded by Osborne Road, St Andrew's Road, Kingfield Road, Cherry Tree Road and Union Road together with Meadow Bank Avenue. Miss Newbould also owned Sharrow Mount, the site of the old workhouse on Psalter Lane, various building plots and houses on Lyndhurst, Wath, Wake, Joshua and Emily Roads and, further afield, property at Attercliffe.

The story of the Newbould family is inextricably mixed with that of other well-known families, the Wilsons of the Snuff Mills, Thomas Holy, buttonmaker, whose works were on The Moor near the present Holy Street, George Wostenholm and the Batties of Sharrow Head House. The first Newbould of whom we have any details is William of Ecclesall Old Hall which was at the top of Millhouses Lane. In addition to farming William owned a small drift mine in the area at the bottom of the present Knowle Lane and it is interesting that later members of the family became involved in coal mining in the Intake area. When William died in 1725, aged forty-seven, his son Thomas inherited the farm which was let. Thomas was apprenticed in 1727 to John Wild, a shearsmith, and then to Thomas Wilson who was the father of the founder of the Snuff Mills on Sharrow Vale Road. Thomas Newbould was made a Freeman of The Cutlers' Company in 1738 and was Master in 1751 at the age of thirty-seven.

Sometime after 1747 Thomas Newbould acquired premises on Coalpit Lane (now Cambridge Street) where he produced various types of edge tools. However, there was no water in the area so products were sent to grinding wheels elsewhere. He then took a lease of the Broomhall Wheel on the River Porter. This had formerly belonged to John Sheldon and was close to the corn mill which had been built by the Jessops before 1630. Both these wheels stood near to the area between Napier Street and Summerfield Street now covered by the

works of SKF and Dormer Tools. In 1784 Thomas's son Samuel transferred the works from Coalpit Lane to the Bridgefield Works. Both works and family house were at the bottom of The Moor near the present South Lane. Samuel had acquired the property from his father-in-law, John Taylor, a carrier. By about 1819 Samuel had acquired twelve acres of land, seven of which are now part of the General Cemetery. Thomas's second son, William, married Sarah, daughter of Thomas Holy, and was in business with him as a buttonmaker. Samuel inherited the family works and in turn became a Freeman of The Cutlers' Company in 1780 and Master in 1800. He lived to be ninety years old and at eighty-two, 'active as ever', was at a ball at Wentworth House. The story of the firm of Samuel Newbould and Company and its growth can be read in the Sanderson Kayser Magazine, vol. 2, no. 5, 1971, and in additional MS material by Colin Cooper. The history of the members of the Newbould family who lived at Broomhill near to the present Newbould Lane is told by Margaret MacKenzie in the Broomhall Magazine, April–May, 1970. We will concentrate on the local Nether Edge side of the family.

On the 4th June 1817 Samuel's third son, Henry, a 'merchant' in the family business, married Mary Williamson of Buntingford, Hertfordshire, and in 1820 he bought a house which he called Sharrow Bank. This is the house at the corner of Cherry Tree Road and Psalter Lane now used as The Handicapped People's Day Centre. The garden of the house was extensive, running right through to the present Clifford Road. At the same time his father-in-law, William Williamson, bought up plots of land at Psalter Lane and Cherry Tree Road adjoining Henry's house. When he made his will in 1829 he left 'Shirl or Shirley Hill' to his daughter for life and after her death to Henry and then to 'all and every or any one or more of the child or children' as either Henry or Mary should direct. When new roads were developed in the area Williamson Road was named after the family and Clifford Road was named after a house opposite to Sharrow Bank belonging to the Wilson family and called Clifford. Over the years the Newbould family played their part in local affairs. Henry and other members of his family were churchwardens, Overseers of the Poor and, later, Guardians of the Poor and during the cholera epidemic of 1831 they were Commissioners appointed to carry out the inspections to see that sanitary precautions were carried out. They, together with members of the Wilson family, were shareholders in the turnpike to Chapel-en-le-Frith which ran via Sharrow Head. In 1798 the tolls taken there amounted to £240. When the turnpike to Glossop was being built Henry was one of the trustees responsible for paying recompense to owners whose land was bought.

For many years Henry Newbould was closely involved with the affairs of the occupants of Sharrow Head House. In 1747 John Battie, an attorney who was 'Steward of the Manor Court', in other words agent for the Lord of the Manor of Ecclesall, made his will. John left the lease of Sharrow Head House and its estate to his younger son William. His will gives a fascinating glimpse of the domestic life of a well-to-do family of that time. In addition to his property, which included the rights to a gallery and seats in the Parish Church of Sheffield, he detailed personal effects such as a silver tankard, a silver pint mug, silver gill mug and little tumbler, silver coffee pot and stand, a great silver stand engraved with the Battie arms, four silver salt cellars, silver tea pot and milk pot, silver sugar castor, 'six new Silver Table Spoons whereon are engraved my Christ [sic] . . .' and a 'fine Diaper Table Cloth and the twelve Napkins thereto . . .'.

Sharrow Head House showing 17th century portion. The larger wing (inset) was built in 1766.

William followed his father's profession of lawyer and was, in turn, agent for the Lord of the Manor, the Marquis of Rockingham. He had an extensive law practice and at one time had sixty-four clients from all parts of the country and financial backgrounds. They included the Reverend James Wilkinson, the Vicar of the Parish Church, Thomas Newbould, William Smith, an ironmonger of the High Street, the Governors of the Sheffield Free School and the Trustees of the Ecclesall Highways. His office was in Paradise Square and was referred to by one writer as 'the nursery of men prominent in the next generation of lawyers'. He bought Sharrow Head House and enlarged it employing the well-known surveyor William Fairbank to oversee the work. In 1766 the enlargement included an office each for William and his clerk, a brew house, a carriage house, a greenhouse and extensive stabling in which, no doubt, he kept the sorrel Galloway and grey gelding which he bequeathed to his brother John in his will. It is of interest that the surveyor William Fairbank ran a school in Coalpit Lane which was attended by Battie and Newbould children. He also attended families in their own home to teach French for which he charged 10s. a quarter plus 8d. a visit.

Neither William nor John married and after William's death his unmarried sisters continued to live in the house. The estate descended to Margaret, daughter of a sister, Susan, who had married Thomas Smith, her brother's client. This Thomas was 'of Sheffield' as distinct from Thomas, his son, who was 'of Dunstan Hall, Chesterfield' which he had 'in the right of his wife' and whose family was to play such a large part in Henry Newbould's life. These well-to-do families would all have met at the various social functions in Sheffield and Susan was 'Queen of the Assembly' at one time.

In 1788 Margaret Smith married the Reverend Alexander MacKenzie, the curate of the Parish Church of Sheffield, and the following year he became Vicar of St Paul's Church which stood on the site of the Peace Gardens. Alexander and Margaret had several children who died young and one daughter, Margaret. After his wife's death in 1793 Alexander married Sarah, daughter of Joseph Wilson and they had a daughter, Mary Ann. His daughter Margaret married a Captain Henry Limbrick Toll of Waterslade, Blackhawton, Devon, a captain in the Devon Militia stationed in Sheffield, and at this time the Newbould family became involved. Henry's cousin, Thomas, who was managing the family business was, at that time, living at Brightfield House (now Charnwood Hotel on Sharrow Lane). He later moved to what is now 21 Cherry Tree Road and was Secretary to The Royal Infirmary. At the time of Margaret's marriage Thomas was one of the trustees of her marriage settlement and after his death in 1844 Henry continued to act as a 'friend' and became increasingly involved in the administration of the Sharrow Head estate.

When Margaret Toll made her will in 1820 she named Henry Newbould as one of her trustees and executors. She directed that £3,000 be invested by them and the interest paid to her half sister Mary Ann until she was twenty-one or was married. The other income from her property should be divided between the children of her uncle Thomas Smith of Dunstan Hall with the exception of the eldest who would inherit the Dunstan Hall estate. After her husband Captain Toll's death and when the oldest cousin reached twenty-one her estate was to be auctioned and the proceeds divided between those cousins. The next year she added a codicil. She left the £3,000 to Mary Ann outright and, on her death in 1821, Mary Ann was declared her next of kin. Mary Ann married William Smith of Barnes Hall, Grenoside, apparently no relation to the other Smiths in the family. Captain Toll did not die until 1844 and by that time there were seven 'Dunstan' Smith cousins and Mary Ann and William Smith of Barnes Hall had eleven children. A complicated case in the Court of Chancery then ensued. This dragged on for several years being complicated by various supplemental pleas, by running out of the allotted time and by Mary Ann having two more children. One of the supplemental pleas was on behalf of the infant children of William 'Dunstan' Smith. Their father had died and their representative, 'their next friend', pleaded that they were entitled to their father's share. Another complication was a plea entered by John MacKenzie, a distant cousin of Mary Ann. He claimed that, through his grandfather, he was Mary Ann's next of kin. However, the plea was refused by the Master of the Chancery Court and finally, in 1847, it was directed that the estate be auctioned and the proceeds divided equally between all the claimants.

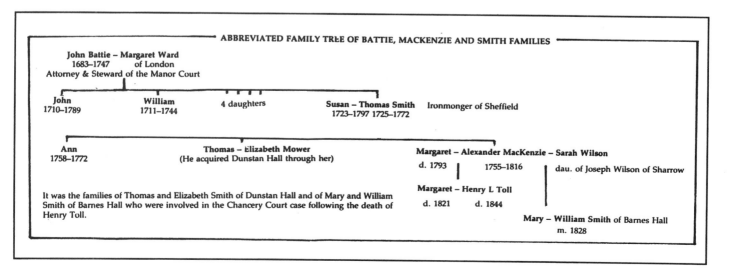

ABBREVIATED FAMILY TREE OF BATTIE, MACKENZIE AND SMITH FAMILIES

John Battie – Margaret Ward
1683–1747 of London
Attorney & Steward of the Manor Court

John 1710–1789 | William 1711–1744 | 4 daughters | Susan – Thomas Smith 1723–1797 1725–1772 Ironmonger of Sheffield

Ann 1758–1772 | Thomas – Elizabeth Mower (He acquired Dunstan Hall through her) | Margaret – Alexander MacKenzie – Sarah Wilson d. 1793 1755–1816 dau. of Joseph Wilson of Sharrow

It was the families of Thomas and Elizabeth Smith of Dunstan Hall and of Mary and William Smith of Barnes Hall who were involved in the Chancery Court case following the death of Henry Toll.

Margaret – Henry L Toll d. 1821 d. 1844

Mary – William Smith of Barnes Hall m. 1828

Henry skilfully negotiated all these legal matters on behalf of the family and managed the sale of the property which was divided into fourteen lots. They covered land from Sharrow Head down Cemetery Road and Sharrow Lane and included land later bought by George Wostenholm for his estate at Kenwood and much of the land bought by Thomas Steade for building plots. Whilst dealing with all these matters Henry had, himself, been buying up a great deal of property in the area. In 1834 he bought the land at Cherry Tree Hill known as King Field and in 1840 he bought land covering the present Osborne Road from John Sheldon. This is the area which runs from Union Road up to the corner of St Andrew's Road and it adjoined the property of John Bright. After the Guardians of the Poor bought land from John Bright for the new Ecclesall Bierlow Workhouse in 1839 Henry sold half of his land, known as 'The Bank', to the Guardians to enable a road to be built. At that time the road was named Workhouse Lane but later changes in attitude caused it to be re-named Osborne Road after two local families. At the same time Henry bought the old workhouse on Psalter Lane (later Sharrow Mount) from the Guardians. In 1846 he bought more land at Cherry Tree Hill from Samuel Greaves and in 1858 he bought Wistaria Cottage and continued to buy up land in and adjoining the present Kingfield Road and Meadow Bank Avenue.

Henry and his wife at Sharrow Bank had four children. William Williamson Newbould, born in 1819, became a clergyman and had six children. When he made his will in 1880 he was described as of Trinity College, Cambridge, but resident in Honington, Warwickshire, and when he died he was in Kew in Surrey. There was a son, Henry, about whom we know only that he lived in Adderbury, Oxfordshire, and died at the early age of thirty-two. The members of the family who continue the family story in Nether Edge were twins, John and Elizabeth, born in 1822. John became a lawyer, being admitted in the Trinity Term, 1848, and had his own firm at 4 Paradise Square and he was agent to the Church of England Insurance Company at 14 Norfolk Street. He was also an auditor of the Sheffield Law Society from its foundation in 1875 until his death in 1880. The 1851 census shows the occupants of

Sharrow Bank to be Henry Newbould (61) landed proprietor, Mary (58), John (28) solicitor, Elizabeth (28) and four servants, one male and three female. After Henry's death in 1871 John and Elizabeth continued to live at Sharrow Bank and the census for 1871 lists John (48) attorney and landowner, Elizabeth, sister, together with a cook, two housemaids and a footman.

John died unmarried and intestate in 1880 and Elizabeth moved to Leamington Spa where she spent the rest of her life and where she had a cousin, Samuel, living. Sharrow Bank was sold and the sale catalogue gives some indication of the lifestyle to which John and Elizabeth were accustomed. The sale lasted for seven days and the first two were devoted solely to the sale of books, prints, engravings and pictures. Over four hundred books showed a catholic taste and included many volumes of botanical and gardening journals, an interest reflected in the exotic camellias, azaleas and other choice plants in the three greenhouses, two stove houses and the fern house. Each plant was named and sold as a separate item. Included in the collection of glass and china were thirty-nine cut-glass finger bowls and forty-three decanters together with spirit bottles and claret jugs. These were matched by the bins of wine, spirits and champagnes in the cellar. Other interests of the family are indicated by 'a box of fossils and an old accordion' in the study and the many books on America show their interest in the travels of other members of the Newbould family who represented the family firm in America.

Elizabeth and her brother William were John's next of kin and, as such, entitled to his property. When William made his will in 1880 he appointed their cousin Samuel his executor and guardian of his children. William died in 1886 and, at that time, there was another Chancery Court case claiming that William had been entitled to one-third of the estate of their father, Henry. The Court case was not settled until 1890 when awards were made to the family of William; in 1892 Elizabeth made various payments to his family and, in 1895, the executors assigned to Elizabeth all that property 'situated in the Township of Sheffield, Brightside Bierlow, Upper Hallam, Nether Hallam, Attercliffe-cum-Darnall and Ecclesall Bierlow, the Parish of Heeley near Sheffield, the Township of Stannington in the Parish of Ecclesfield. Also in the Parish of Great Hormead in the County of Hereford.'

Sale Plan of Sharrow Bank, 1881.

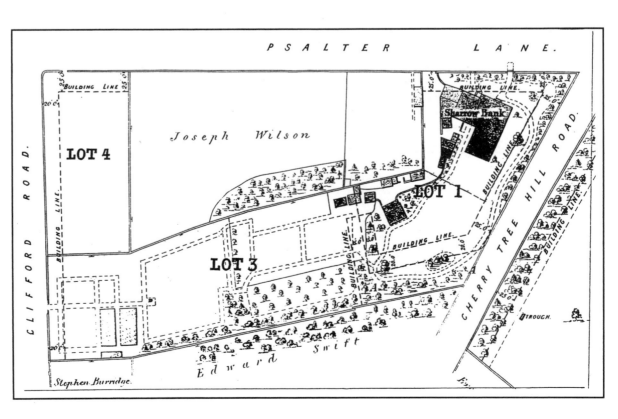

In addition to the extensive property which Elizabeth inherited she and her cousin, Samuel, although living in Leamington Spa, had retained their interest in property in Nether Edge. In 1884 Elizabeth bought virtually all the land now bounded by Machon Bank Road (the lower part of Osborne Road was not yet built), Ladysmith Avenue, Edgebrook Road and Union Road whilst Samuel bought up the leases of several of the remaining pieces of land. This included The Edge and its then extensive grounds on Ladysmith Avenue. In 1897 Elizabeth sold part of the land to a builder, Henry Brumby, and it was typical of the family's care for their property that she laid down stringent conditions for the type of property to be built. The houses, walls, etc were all to be to her satisfaction or that of her heirs and to be in good condition at all times. Private houses were to be built of a minimum value of £200 and they were to be stone faced and not more than two storeys high, all out-buildings were to be screened from the roads.

When Elizabeth made her will in 1903 she appointed her friends Alfred and Ernest Maxwell, solicitors, Joshua Wortly, chartered accountant (at that time living at 5 Kingfield Road), and her nephews William Henry, banker's assistant living in New Zealand, and Newton John, surgeon, of Childe Okeford, Blandford, Dorset, as her executors. However, William Henry's appointment was to be invalid unless he returned to England and notified the trustees that he intended to reside permanently in England. He appears not to have done this and when Elizabeth died in Leamington Spa on the 27th April 1909, it was Newton John who administered the sale of the estate with the other executors. Elizabeth was buried at Ecclesall Church on 1st May 1909.

Sale of contents of Sharrow Bank, 1881.

The Last Remains of Upper Edge

Upper Edge was a prosperous and extensive farmstead dating from late medieval times, which stood on what is now Oakdale Road. The numerous buildings stretched from Union Road down to the present Fountside flats (which themselves stand on the site of the former 'Manor House' — a Victorian mansion demolished in the 1960s). This small piece of buttressed wall — about 400 years old — stands unobtrusively in the car park at the rear of Fountside and is all that remains of 'Upper Edge'.

The Wilsons and the Snuff Mill

◆ Susan Cleary

There can be few families or commercial concerns who can trace their roots back as far as the Wilson family of Sharrow are able to do. The geography of the area has changed radically since Joseph Wilson first appeared on the scene, but the business of Wilsons & Co (Sharrow) Ltd; Snuff Manufacturers and Exporters, still retains an old fashioned image.

Joseph Wilson is generally regarded as the founder of the Snuff Mill at Sharrow but the family connection arose in the area before this time. Joseph's father, Thomas Wilson, came to Sharrow in 1737, leasing the water wheel on the Porter Brook from the Duke of Norfolk. Thomas was a shearsmith and edge tool maker of Fargate. After Thomas died in 1740 his youngest son Joseph introduced the art of snuff making to Sheffield. The methods and processes which he developed are still employed today. He started with the sum of £1,900 from his father's estate and laid the foundations of the business. Joseph was also a silversmith, plater and saw-maker.

Joseph married Ann, daughter of George Greaves of Sheffield in about 1752. The couple probably lived in Norfolk Street to begin with but the family moved to Highfield House on Sharrow Lane in about 1766. This house still exists today as the Charnwood Hotel. They had thirteen children in all, eight of whom survived.

Joseph appeared to be a rather fickle businessman. As many of the old account papers show, he often lent money which was never repaid and his accounts rarely balanced. He appeared to be frequently fobbed off whilst trying to collect debts from his clients. Joseph was made bankrupt in 1775 and relatives of the family had to rally round to pay his debts of £1,450 and enable his business to continue trading. At this time Joseph's diverse interests were sold off in favour of his snuff business. Joseph was released from bankruptcy in 1778. Joseph's son, Joseph Jr, joined the business in 1775. He began by travelling, calling on customers, taking orders and collecting accounts. Joseph Jr's brother Thomas joined the business in 1783, also beginning by travelling.

In 1788 a family agreement concerning ownership of the business was made, basically deciding that the running of the business was to be left to the three brothers, Joseph Jr, Thomas and William, 'the House of Joseph, Thomas and William Wilson'. From this time on Joseph Snr was not in good relations with his sons, and he later left Sheffield for London where he set up house with a Mrs Deborah Andrews, a former employee. He attempted to establish a snuff business there, apparently unsuccessfully. Joseph's wife Ann, meanwhile, continued to live at Highfield with the sons mainly living at Sharrow Mill, their house being kept by one of their sisters, whilst the remaining sisters lived at Highfield. Highfield is a mere ten minutes walk from the Mills; in the late 1700s it is likely that walkers would walk along the Porter Brook and cut across fields between the two.

Ann Wilson died in 1795 at Highfield, but Joseph did not return to Sheffield due to his own ill health. She was buried at St Paul's Church (now the site of the Peace Gardens), as were many previous and subsequent Wilsons. Shortly after Ann's death Joseph and Deborah were married on 28th December. Nine days later Joseph made his last will and the next day he died aged 73. A disputed portion of the business, which Joseph's sons had never paid to their father was not paid to his widow either. Deborah disputed the sons' action by a 'sute in Chancery', but it appears that the action was unsuccessful.

In 1794, with the business appearing to be successful after the effects of the bankruptcy, Joseph Jr purchased land at Sharrow Head and Westbrook House was built. Accounts existing show that ale was given to the tradesmen at the completion of each stage of work: 'foundation ale', 'flooring ale', 'stare case ale', and 'roofing ale'.

Highfield was sold to Joseph Ibberson for £1,020 in 1798, the family living henceforward at the Mill or Westbrook.

During the years following the Mill was extended. In June 1799 'Foundation Ale' was paid for the enlargement of the Big Room. Shortly after 'Gave Peter two pints of Ale (4d.) for Hanging the stone', and the joiners were soon sitting down to their 'Flooring Ale'. The counting house was also enlarged and all the adjacent part of the building was brought into the form which it presents today. During the years 1807–10 the Stable, Barn and Cooper's Shop, the bridge and the river wall were built. In 1812 the Porter's Lodge was erected and in 1819 the Cart 'Shead', followed by the Chaise House in 1825.

The Mill House at Sharrow, home and place of work to generations of Wilsons.

Grinding tobacco leaf to make snuff in the original water-powered mill.

Much land was also acquired during this period. The Mill, Tom Cross Farm and the Dam Field were purchased from the Duke of Norfolk in 1798. Shortly after, land on Brincliffe Edge was purchased. Endcliffe Farm and four others were purchased in 1810, followed by two of the Porter Brook water wheels, the Endcliffe and Stalker Wheels. The use of the wheels was let to a number of small mesters who rented one or more troughs, names of those tenants include Danl. Brammall, Thos. Wild, Saml. Dyson, Saml. Blagdon, Jno. Sanderson, Wm. Beardshaw & Sons, Jno. Cartledge, W. Ibbotson, Abraham Bradshaw Abraham Bocking, Jonathan Beet, James Wostenholme, Joseph Hibberson.

Most of the land and property purchased up to 1810 was the subject of a Deed of Partition in 1813. Under this, Joseph took the land mostly to the east of the Mill (Sharrow Head, Westbrook and parts of Sharrow Moor, also Stalker Wheel). Joseph was later to extend his land to Abbeydale and Millhouses by purchasing the Holt House Estate for £9,108. William's share mostly to the west extended to Hunters Bar and up Brocco Bank, and included Endcliffe Wheel. Thomas had land on Sharrow Moor to the south including Cherry Tree Hill, Shirle Hill and Hunter's Farm, also land between Psalter Lane and what is now Sharrow Vale Road, and from the present Clifford School to Bagshot Street, and here Thomas built his house Clifford. Building accounts include 'George Gregory diging foundations 11/8d', 'Thos Boot laying Causeway 3/9d'.

Employees during these years earned their wage, and were certainly poles apart from their employers. Odd perks to the job included the annual Fish Feast, All Saints Day — where women and children received 2d and 1d respectively, Easter and Christmas gifts, also help when illness struck. Drink money was another 'perk' paid at various times, eg 'Drying Ale' was regularly paid to men engaged on turning hot tobacco.

By the time Joseph Jr and Thomas died various children were working in the business, Joseph (III), Henry and Francis, sons of Joseph Jr, and their cousins George and William (II). The two sets of cousins frequently disagreed and in 1831 a new Mill was built above Westbrook House, Westbrook Mill. Sharrow Mills remained in the hands of William Wilson and his sons William and George. The new business at Westbrook Mill emerged as the house of Joseph and Henry Wilson. At the same time the two concerns agreed to split their trading areas. The oral agreement lasted until 1913. Joseph and Henry Wilson and their descendants continued to run Westbrook or 'Top' Mill until 1953 when, with no-one to carry on the business in the family, the Imperial Tobacco Company took it over. The snuff at the two mills, whilst both being of a high quality, has always differed slightly.

William Wilson was followed by four more William Wilsons in direct descent, while his second son, George, established the other line, hence the title 'Wilsons & Co'.

William and his family lived at Sharrow Mills until 1819. Aged fifty-four he had for some years discontinued the practice of working in the morning. He had a trapdoor constructed in the wall of his bedroom through which he pushed the key to the Mills, down a chute, to the waiting foreman each morning. In 1819 William moved to the house on Sharrow Lane (opposite Highfield) now known as Mount Pleasant. He rode to work on a horse from here.

William and his wife Mary Ann had eleven children but only the sons William (II) and George consistently worked in the business. They both invested heavily the profits of the Mill, at least until the time of their respective marriages. Local investments included local enterprises such as the Gas and Water Companies, Sheffield Cotton Mill Company, Sheffield Banking Company and the Botanical Gardens. Investments further afield included the various railway companies.

William had a retiring nature, whilst George was a more outgoing character. They both lived frugally as had their father and uncles. Both brothers were aged fifty when they married. Their only interest outside work before this time was sport, both hunted, but George preferred to shoot.

William (II) and his wife Hannah lived at Whitely Wood before moving to The Moss, Dore. A great walker, for many years he walked to and from the Mills every day. Their children were William (III), Mary and Thomas.

George and his wife Emily lived at The Mount, Broomhill, at that time a 'terrace' of seven houses, in two of the houses knocked into one. The view across the moors was unbroken at this time. In fact The Mount was spoken of as 'Flockton's Folly' because it was considered so far out of Sheffield that no-one would ever want to live there. Children born to the couple were George, John, Emily, Selina and Thomas. George continued to invest heavily after his marriage and in 1867 he purchased Tapton Hall for £3,500, paying a further £1,424 for furniture and £218 for wine.

George died in 1878 and at this time William retired from the business, living a further nine years. George's son George Kingsford and William (II)'s son William (III) took over at Sharrow Mill.

William and George both made large fortunes and were the last generation to escape the impact of surtax. The extent of their wealth is evident from William (II)'s will, 'an annuity of £5,000 for his wife, £200,000 to be invested for his daughter, as well as the lion's share which went to his sons'.

William Wilson (III) and George Kingsford Wilson were aged twenty-eight and twenty-five respectively when they took over in 1878. William (III) married Fanny and lived at Beauchief Abbey and children born to them who survived were William (IV), Winifred and twins May and Violet. A keen shot, he owned Stanedge and Hallam Moors, and he was also a keen huntsman. He died in 1927.

George married Florence Dixon of neighbouring Stumperlowe Hall. (Florence's sister Beatrice married Thomas, brother of George. Mrs Beatrice Wilson never used a motor car and her carriage and pair were a familiar sight in Sheffield until her death in 1947. She was once heard to remark, 'the Wilsons never talk of anything but Shooting and Shares'.) George and Florence's children were George, Ronald, Henry and Vera. Like his father, George did not interest himself in public affairs and had no desire for personal aggrandizement. A Government envoy was quickly shown the door when it became apparent that he was being offered a baronetcy in return for (to George) merely 'small change'. He had a deep distrust of Government Departments as is indicated by his refusal to deal with official forms. Forms sent to him for completion were returned a year later marked 'illegal'. He died in 1933 aged eighty and, in accordance with old custom, his coffin was carried by six snuff-grinders.

Prior to the deaths of William (III) and George Kingsford, the Mill was being run by William (IV) and Ronald, their fathers being in semi-retirement. During the First World War both young men went into the Army, their places being taken by May and Violet. The flavouring of snuff and the treatment of the tobacco requires considerable physical effort (two tons of tobacco must be turned with a hay fork in one part of the secret process) and these two ladies carried out this arduous duty regularly for several years. They both, with Winifred, enjoyed hunting. Violet died while hunting. May lived until the mid-1960s.

William (IV) married Margery of Totley Hall and their children were Elsie, William (V) and Anne. William (V) entered the business in 1932 and died in 1944 whilst in the RAF. Thus ended the male line of William Wilson of Sharrow after nearly two centuries. Ronald Wilson never married. He died suddenly at Tapton in 1958.

The business was incorporated as a Limited Company in 1952 and thus began modernisation. Pre-packaged goods dominate. Old flavours have been revived and new ones introduced, particularly in the field of medicated snuffs. New machines were necessary and in 1954 a new building was erected to house them. The basis of the trade remains unchanged. The bulk of sales is still of SP snuffs, ground on the same mills (now electrically driven) and sent out in the same two, one or half pound canisters of yore. SS snuff remains the second favourite and is still ground on the water wheel. The introduction of a typewriter in 1955 was regarded as revolutionary by some of Wilsons' older customers who wrote, more in sorrow than in anger, to protest at this sign of the changing times. Since 1953 when increased competition existed due to Westbrook Mill being taken over by the Imperial Tobacco Company, old customs have had to be replaced. Such changes include advertising. The present owners of the Mill all remain as direct descendants of Joseph Wilson.

Blending snuff in the cellars of the Mill House, according to a time-honoured recipe.

Public service and private profit

◆ Shirley Meek

a Cautionary Tale of Early Nineteenth Century Ecclesall

The old workhouse of Ecclesall Bierlow, built in 1793 at Sharrow Mount on Psalter Lane. After the new workhouse opened in 1844 it was converted into private housing, and was finally demolished in the 1960s.

In 1808 the township of Ecclesall Bierlow had a population of about 6,000. It was still mainly a rural area, stretching from the edge of Sheffield town out to the villages of Heeley and Whirlow. The people who lived there were mostly employed in agriculture, or made their living in the small forges and smithies attached to their cottages. If they became sick or destitute, and were unable to provide for themselves, they could apply to the Overseers of the Poor of the Township for 'out-relief' or to be admitted to the workhouse on Sharrow Moor. The necessary money was raised by the Poor Rate levied on all property in the district. The Overseers were gentlemen, 'substantial householders and fit and proper persons' who were elected by the ratepayers to serve, unpaid, for a year at a time.

In the same way the roads in the Township were looked after by the elected Surveyors of the Highways, who also levied rates or could require larger property owners to provide labourers for work on the roads.

As the Overseers and the Surveyors were gentlemenly amateurs they depended heavily on paid assistants to do most of the actual work. These were the Collector of the Rates, the Assistant to the Surveyors, the Assistant to the Overseers and the Vestry Clerk. The term 'Vestry' was applied to the ratepayers of the Township or their elected representatives, no doubt because their meetings had originally taken place in the vestry of the church. Frequently one man held two or more of these posts at the same time. The pay was not high, but as we shall see the opportunities for lining one's pockets were considerable. Whether the system worked efficiently or not depended on the conscientiousness of the gentlemen who were nominally in charge, and on the honesty of their employees.

The Minutes of the Proceedings at Vestry Meetings of Ecclesall Bierlow (1808 to 1857) from which I have taken most of the material for this account, open in 1808 with the declaration: 'It is the opinion of this meeting that the Overseers have done perfectly right in dismissing William Bradshaw from his employment of Collecting the Poor Rates.' No reason is given, but one can hazard a guess from the stipulation that applicants for the post 'will be expected to devote the whole of their time to the Parish Business as required and to give security to the township. No person need apply who is not forty years of age.' Mr Luke Cadman was appointed as the new Collector, and at the same time Mr John Ellin was granted a sum of 40 guineas as a reward 'for his assiduity and attention as agent and assistant to the Overseers of the Poor'. (Later, 1810, John Ellin's salary was raised to 60 guineas and Luke Cadman's to £50 per annum.)

In 1809 it was the turn of the Surveyors of the Highways to get into trouble with the ratepayers. It was voted unanimously that 'Mr Thomas Smith, as Assistant to the Surveyors, had been negligent in his said office and that his further assistance be dispensed with'. A long list of conditions to be followed by future Surveyors was laid down, which makes it all too clear what had been going on: 'No ale to be allowed to any labourers, and only one pint shall be allowed to a person who drives a team with one labourer and two pints to the team that furnishes two labourers'. 'No paupers to be suffered to work at Salter Lane Delf, except Christopher Taylor will pay their wages' (obviously Thomas Smith had been doing very nicely by providing unpaid pauper labour at the stone quarries on Brincliffe Edge, presumably with the connivance of the Workhouse Governor?). And a long list of local worthies set their hands to the declaration 'that if the present or any future Surveyors shall deviate from the foregoing Resolutions we pledge ourselves that we will appear and vote against their Rate'.

After this no more scandals surfaced for several years. John Ellin, the Vestry Clerk, retired and was succeeded in 1822 by James Richardson. James' spelling was erratic and during his time in office the Township minutes are untidy with many crossings out and alterations. However the ratepayers were satisfied enough to resolve unanimously in 1825 that 'the building of a house for the Vestry Clerk, he paying a proper rent for the same, the house to be built on the Township lands, to be agreed to'. This house was built on Psalter Lane, at the entrance to the Ecclesall Bierlow Workhouse which many people will still remember as Sharrow Mount, and is the building known as 110 Psalter Lane.

Between 1826 and 1829 there are very few entries in the Minute Book, not more than one page for each year. James Richardson does not appear to have been doing any more than recording the annual meetings at which the Surveyors and the Overseers were elected. In May 1830, however, we find out how he had really been occupied: 'At a meeting of the ratepayers to pass the accounts of the late Overseers, it appeared there was a Ballance of £328.2.8 due from James Richardson the Vestry Clerk, for which the meeting agreed to take his joint note with Mr Rbt Dent, payable in installments by £50 per year'. How he proposed to do this out of a salary of about £60 per year is not stated, nor why one of the retiring Overseers was willing to share the responsibility for payment.

This attempted cover-up did not satisfy all the ratepayers, though. Fourteen of them requested a further public meeting to examine the accounts more closely, as it seemed that only some of the books had so far been checked. The minutes of this meeting occupy several pages.

A committee of five local worthies, including Mr John Brown, Mr James Dixon and Mr Joseph Mappin jnr was appointed 'under whose direction the accounts were to be fully investigated and the true balance ascertained, and who should assist the Overseers, Mr Robert Dent and Mr William Tyzack, in the discharge of their duties'. Further resolutions were:

'That inasmuch as the Vestry Clerk is in so great a Defalcation it is the opinion of this meeting that Mr James Richardson be no longer continued in such a situation, and that the Overseers dismiss him forthwith from every office and situation which he fills and occupies in the Township affairs.

'That the offices of Vestry Clerk and Collector of rates be no longer suffered to be held by the same person.

'That the salary of the Vestry Clerk in future be £60 a year, with the occupation of the house in which Mr Richardson lives free from rent and taxes, and that he gives sufficient security for the Discharge of his Office.

'That George Knowles be appointed Collector of the Rates with an allowance of £2 per cent on the net amount collected, but without any other allowance.

'That the thanks of this meeting be given to the Requisitionists for calling it, and the Parties to the paper signed A Rate Payer, and that the expense of printing be paid by the Overseers out of the Parish Funds.'

The Committee soon found that the task of cleaning up the Township's financial affairs was no easy one. The Overseers put up a brisk rearguard action, refusing to dismiss James Richardson until all the books had been audited; but the Committee reported 'we had reason to believe that these accounts are in many instances false and fraudulent, inasmuch as many entries have been altered since your Committee were appointed, to the injury of the Ratepayers generally'. Only when the Committee threatened to resign en bloc did the Overseers agree to dismiss Richardson and to co-operate in the full investigation of the accounts.

Heads continued to roll as these investigations went on. George Knowles lasted barely eight weeks in his new post: 'In consequence of the Collector, George Knowles, delivering his books of accounts in such an improper state and on being remonstrated with, his answers being so very unsatisfactory, we think it proper in justice to the Township that he be immediately discharged from his office'. It seems unlikely that he could have got away with much money in such a short time in the current glare of publicity, so perhaps he had already had his fingers in the till during James Richardson's period of office, and was trying to hide his tracks?

'We also agree that Mrs Naylor be discharged from her situation as Governess of the Poorhouse forthwith in consequence of a variety of misconduct on her part too numerous to relate' (but how I wish we had been given some details!).

The final report of the Committee's investigations runs to many pages of the Minute Book, and I can only pick out a few excerpts:

'The Bastardy accounts were in a very shameful state, indeed many of them had not been posted up into the ledger for 2 years, and some for 3, 4, 5, 6 and even 7 years which caused a great many of the accounts to be disputed and will be a certain and serious loss to the Township'. These were the accounts presented to the fathers of bastard children, who were required to pay something towards their upkeep by the Township. 'One instance will illustrate this, the Bastardy account of a Grocer was allowed to accumulate to near £18 altho' the Overseers were at the same time paying the Individual large sums of money for groceries and a short time back he scheduled the parish out of £14.10.0.'.

'In looking over the rate-books we found them in such a disgraceful state that it was not safe to start the Collector with such a book' so that a revaluation of property was undertaken, 'and we are sorry to add that Property was found which had never been entered in the rate-book'.

'It appears therefore that there has not only been a great and wilfull negligence on James Richardson's part in the Township affairs, but also gross fraud by alterations made by him in a variety of instances in the account books by totally omitting in many cases to debit himself with large sums admitted by him to have been received'.

The Committee concludes by recommending that legal proceedings should be instituted against him for fraud. Even more important was the recommendation that 'the Township should invariably appoint a committee to investigate the accounts ere they are submitted to the Parishioners if they wish to avoid such mistakes in future'. A lot of trouble might indeed have been avoided if this advice had been taken, and if the future ratepayers had been prepared to display the same 'indefatigable zeal and talent in the investigation of the accounts of this Township' as that Committee of 1830.

Bringing James Richardson to justice proved a difficult task, though. Four months later there is a note of a meeting attended by the Chapelwarden and the Overseers but only two members of the Committee, at which 'Mr Benjamin Burbeary read to the meeting the letter addressed to him by Mr Luke Palfreyman as solicitor for Mr James Richardson'. The contents are not mentioned.

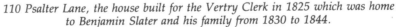

110 Psalter Lane, the house built for the Vertry Clerk in 1825 which was home to Benjamin Slater and his family from 1830 to 1844.

'Resolved: that Mr Burbeary have authority to take the best security he can obtain from Mr Richardson and to settle the matter in dispute between the latter and the Township in such a manner as he may deem most advisable.'

This further attempt to cover up caused an explosion. At the foot of the page, in another hand, is written 'PS Query — How was this meeting got up? For what purpose? And what did Mr Palfreyman's letter contain? To say the least of the above it was not Gentlemanly Conduct to the rest of the Committee who were not invited to the meeting. Jn Brown, who was not aware of it'.

And written across the minutes, in red ink: 'I, as one of the Committee do object to the following resolutions as not having notice of the meeting! Jos Mappin jnr'.

All the same, more than two months later the Committee was still resolving to 'wait upon Mr Burbeary to know how he was proceeding with the affairs relating to James Richardson' and 'upon Mr John Watson for his advice as to the steps to be taken against George Knowles or his sureties'. They adjourned the meeting for a few days to report back on these visits to the lawyers. Total silence then descends on the matter and there is no further mention of legal proceedings against anyone. I am forced to wonder just how many others were involved in the scandal, and whether Richardson and Knowles ensured their immunity from prosecution by threatening to name publicly a few worthy gentlemen who had at least been guilty of gross negligence and perhaps of rather more serious offences.

In the meantime, however, a new era had dawned in the Township's affairs. On 16th July 1830 a meeting of the Overseers of the Poor and the Committee, unanimous for once, resolved that 'after hearing the different candidates Mr Benjamin Slater (late of Sheffield but now of Leeds) be appointed to fill the situation of Vestry Clerk at a salary of £100 per annum, with the House and Garden (built for Mr Richardson) free of Rent and Taxes'.

Shortly afterwards Mr Thomas Dewhirst was appointed Governor of the Workhouse and Collector of the Poor Rates and Mrs Dewhirst Governess of the Workhouse. The salaries for each post were £50 per annum, and Mr Dewhirst had to find security for £400 on taking up the appointment.

Benjamin Slater does not seem to have been required to give any financial security, which is surprising after all that had happened recently. He was also very young for the post, being not more than twenty-three when appointed, although he was already a married man with a baby son. He must have made a very favourable impression at the interview to have been given the increased salary of £100 per annum, and certainly the Minute Book immediately shows the presence of a highly efficient and intelligent man. Accounts of meetings are immaculately written up in a beautiful copper-plate hand, and his grammar and spelling are faultless. It is to Benjamin Slater that we owe the detailed accounts of the meetings at which his predecessor's years of fraud were uncovered. However, he did *not* take the minutes at that meeting from which John Brown and Joseph Mappin were excluded.

For the next thirteen and a half years Benjamin Slater was to look after the affairs of Ecclesall Bierlow as the Vestry Clerk, and to be regarded as a public servant of the highest calibre and the most unimpeachable probity.

His capacities were certainly tested in that first year of office. 1831 was census year, and the work of obtaining, collating and recording the information required was all carried out by Slater. This census was not nearly as detailed as those of following years, but it did contain the numbers of houses and of families in Ecclesall Bierlow, the numbers of male and female inhabitants, and a breakdown of the occupations of all working males. As the total population in 1831 was 14,279 compared to a mere 9,113 in 1821 this must have entailed considerable powers of organisation and a great deal of sheer hard work before he could write with pride: 'I Benjamin Slater, a substantial householder in the Township of

Ecclesall Bierlow, do swear that the above report contains, to the best of my knowledge and belief, a full and true answer to the questions contained to the schedule to the Act'.

An interesting light on those early years of Sheffield's expansion to the west is shed by this question and answer in the report:

Q. 'To what do you attribute any remarkable difference in numbers at present, compared to numbers in 1821?'

A. 'The most healthy end of the manufacturing town of Sheffield.'

A much heavier load lay ahead, however, with the outbreak of the Asian Cholera in the town. Some realisation of the Township's responsibility in dealing with infectious diseases is seen in April 1831 when 'in consequence of Charles Wigfall, a poor person admitted into the Poorhouse, seized with Typhus Fever, it is strongly recommended by Mr Wright (the Township Surgeon) and resolved by us that a fever ward be built partly over the surgery now erecting at the Poorhouse'.

Whether any action on these lines had been taken seems doubtful when, in October 1831, cases of cholera appeared at Sunderland, brought by a ship from Hamburg and part of a great pandemic spreading out from India. In mid-November a Township Committee was set up to co-operate with the Sheffield Board of Health. This was a large body consisting of the local Anglican clergy, the Dissenting ministers, the Overseers of the Poor, the Surveyors of Highways and many of the great and good, including four Newboulds and three Wilsons. These gentlemen resolved that the Overseers of the Poor should provide out of the Poor Rates lime and brushes for whitewashing the houses of the poorer classes, also to give 1s. to each inhabitant whose house was cleaned and whitewashed to their satisfaction. The Surveyors' attention was called to the need for removal of nuisances from roads and streets under their care, especially Young Street, Coalpit Lane and Wilkinson Street which had been reported to the committee as some of the most obnoxious parts of the Township, and it was recommended that the state of the sewers be strictly examined.

It is important to remember that Ecclesall Bierlow reached right down to Sheffield Moor, and by now included many overcrowded, festering courts with no proper sanitation and a contaminated water supply.

A few days later gentlemen were appointed as Inspectors, each responsible for a small area of the Township. Their duties were to 'inspect the houses and yards of the Lower Class of Inhabitants, furnish materials for whitewashing, leave a Form offering a reward of 1/- to such poor as are not in circumstances, or cannot be induced, to clean their own houses, and to take minutes of yards that want cleansing and of Poor that require clothing, and to make their report to B Slater, secretary to the Committee'.

Over the next month or two Benjamin Slater was kept very busy trying to get householders to abate nuisances. For example, we find him instructed to wait upon two doctors and ask them to inspect a tan yard in Green Street (off Moore Street) which had occasioned several complaints. It is good to read in March 1832 that he was presented with a gratuity of £10 for 'the very diligent and satisfactory manner in which he had discharged the duties of his office'.

In the middle of this emergency he was also instructed 'to ascertain what rent the property in Spring Street lately assigned by Jas Richardson yields, the terms of lease, what mortgage is on the property, what ground rent, and what quantity of vacant land', and then 'the property to be advertised for sale by public auction'. So perhaps the Township did benefit by some out-of-court and discreet settlement, and was able to recoup part, at least, of the money embezzled.

Unfortunately the Committee's touching faith in limewash as a preventative against the cholera was not justified, and by July 1832 the epidemic was at its height. It is recorded that 1,347 people were taken ill in Sheffield, and 402 of them died including the Master Cutler. Most were buried in

The Cholera Monument marks the mass graves of the victims of the 1832 epidemic.

mass graves in the Cholera Gardens on Norfolk Road, on the hill above the railway station, where the Cholera Monument stands to this day. In the crisis of this epidemic the officers of Ecclesall and Sheffield Townships seem to have made a real attempt to work together, although there was a certain amount of wrangling over the share of the bill which Ecclesall should be expected to pay.

By the next year the cholera had burnt itself out, but some idea that the rapidly increasing population needed a better and purer water supply had obviously penetrated, although it was to be another 20 years before the connection between cholera and a contaminated water source was definitely established. In 1834 Ecclesall Township made a lengthy enquiry into the state of all the public wells and water supplies in the Bierlow and Benjamin Slater was kept busy, among all his other tasks, in such errands as waiting upon the Wilsons to ensure that the public still had access to a well which was now in the extended Snuff Mill Grounds and causing a well near Sharrow Moor School to be cleansed and put into proper repair again.

In the same year there was considerable in-fighting among the ratepayers about the salaries of the Vestry Clerk and the Collector of Rates. An increase was first proposed and then voted down. This must have been galling for Slater after all he had done for the Township, though later in 1834 a lengthy

report detailed the ways in which he had saved considerable sums of money by reducing the numbers of poor persons receiving relief, and the ratepayers did finally agree to raise his salary to £130 per annum.

All the time the population of the Township was increasing as Sheffield expanded to the west. It reached a total of 19,984 at the time of the 1841 census. The demands on the Overseers of the Poor for relief also mounted, as trade was often very bad in the 1830s. In 1834 the Poor Law Amendment Act was passed, and although this measure was unpopular locally and only slowly brought into force, by 1837 the movement to cut down on 'out-relief' and force the destitute, sick and aged into workhouses had started with the setting up of the Ecclesall Bierlow Union. This was an amalgamation for poor relief purposes of Ecclesall Bierlow, Nether and Upper Hallam, and the Derbyshire parishes of Norton, Beauchief and Dore and Totley. The old workhouse on Sharrow Moor was now quite inadequate, so in 1839 the Board of Guardians bought the land on which the new workhouse (later Nether Edge Hospital) was built between 1841 and 1844. This was a huge undertaking financially, costing about £15,000 to build.

By 1841 Benjamin Slater had become the Superintendent Registrar and Vestry and Highway Clerk for Ecclesall Bierlow and the Union Clerk and Assistant Overseer for Ecclesall Bierlow and Nether and Upper Hallam. He was later said to have had a staff of eight clerks under him. There had obviously been a vast increase in both the volume of work and in the sums of money being handled since he was first appointed as Vestry Clerk in 1830.

It is hardly surprising that the Minute Book was no longer being kept in such loving detail as it had been in his first seven or eight years of office, but I do regret that no echoes of local unrest at the time of the abortive Chartist uprising are to be found in the bare and dull records of ratepayers' meetings for 1840.

There are no entries at all between March 1843 and 25th March 1844 but on the latter date, after routine minutes of elections for Overseers of the Poor and the Board of Directors for repair of highways, a bombshell explodes: 'It was passed unanimously that the Overseers of the Poor be requested to call a meeting of the ratepayers of this Township, to be holden at the workhouse on the 8th day of April next, for the purpose of reporting the state of the late Mr Benj. Slater's accounts.'

Benjamin Slater had died on 17th February 1844, after a very short illness, at the age of not more than 36. He left a widow, Ann, and four children, Charles Joseph, 13, Caroline, 12, Anne Eliza, 9, and the baby Henry who had been born some time in 1843.

Mr Samuel Mitchell was employed by the Overseers to carry out an investigation into the accounts of Ecclesall Bierlow and Nether and Upper Hallam, and on 8th April his report was read out to a packed Public Vestry Meeting at the old Sharrow Moor workhouse. It is very lengthy and detailed, but here are some of the most striking excerpts:

'Gentlemen,

Having been requested by you to examine the accounts of the late Mr Slater, your assistant overseer, and to ascertain the deficiency, if any, which might exist therein; and if no such deficiency existed, to clear his previously unimpeached character from the suspicions resting upon it at his Death: . . . I have instituted a careful and most rigid enquiry into the whole of the case.

It is with much pain that I am compelled, from the documents laid before me, to report that the charges of Malversation and fraud in the mode of keeping his Accounts are but too well founded; and that he is greatly in debt to each of the Townships of the District under his Superintendance.'

After making it plain that he is by no means sure that he has uncovered the full extent of the fraud, he concludes that:

'The nett deficiency of Mr Benj. Slater's accounts may be deemed, as far as I know, to be £1,181.10.8½.

It is proper to remark, that this embezzlement of the Public Monies is not a matter of recent occurrence, but has been carried on with great adroitness for a series of years.'

One can imagine the shock felt by the meeting as the corruption of a trusted and respected public servant was revealed. Did some of the older ratepayers feel a sense of déjà vu? The response, anyway, was the same as it had been 14 years earlier; a Committee of five was set up to enquire into the accounts of Mr Slater and of the Overseers, and then report back to a ratepayers' meeting.

On 18th July 1844, this meeting took place at the old workhouse, but was immediately adjourned until 22nd July 'to be holden in the large room attached to the highway office in Eldon Street at 12 o'clock at noon'. Presumably the crowd of ratepayers was too great to be accommodated in the Sharrow Moor premises.

At this point I could hardly wait to read what happened next, and to see what revelations were still to come. I turned the page of the Minute Book . . . and there was nothing. No account was to be found of the postponed meeting; the next entry was a notice of a Vestry meeting to be held on 25th March 1845.

Entry from the Minute Book in which Benjamin Slater records his successful efforts to keep down the rates by decreasing the numbers of those receiving Poor Relief.

This seemed such an extraordinary omission that I looked carefully at the book to see if a page had fallen out. It seemed not, until I realised that on the opposite side of the binding, where a loose page would have been, two pages had been most carefully stuck together to hide the removal of the page with the account of the meeting! It had been expertly done, and part of the entry for 18th July must have been recopied after the page had been taken out.

Most fortunately the reporter of the *Sheffield and Rotherham Independent* was present at that meeting on 22nd July, and the issue of 27th July carries a full and lengthy account of what took place. Reading it I can see exactly why someone preferred to remove all trace of the proceedings from the Minute Book.

The first point to emerge is that Benjamin Slater was very unlucky in being taken ill so suddenly and dying so quickly (he was at work in the office on Monday, by Thursday night 'his illness had assumed a dangerous character', and he died on the Friday). If he had had more time, it seems likely that he would have managed to cover his tracks as successfully as he had done earlier. In November 1843, it came out at the meeting, the auditor Mr Wilkinson 'had discovered that Slater had erased in the books the 4 in an entry of £488 received. He waited on Slater, who said it was a mistake, but he would make all right; and in January Slater did make up the deficiency so as to complete the audit of the previous quarter. He did not communicate this fact until after Slater's decease'. (One wonders what inducement was offered to him to keep the matter dark.) It is hardly surprising that when the Committee started its enquiries Mr Wilkinson first said that he did not know where to find the books he had examined, and later refused to have any minutes made of his statements.

After this, accusations began to fly. Slater's defalcations were due to his having complete control of the collection of the rates; paupers had been employed in making private roads without accounting for their labour; excessively large sums had been paid to Mr Flockton (this was William Flockton, the well-known local architect who had recently designed the new Workhouse) and to others for valuation of property; the

Overseers had at first refused to allow the Committee to examine the account books, and had then availed themselves of professional assistance in their discussions with the Committee 'which showed a hostile spirit', and in the process had run up a large legal bill; and the Overseers and Guardians would only attend their Wednesday meetings if a dinner was provided for them.

'Mr Schofield thought the Guardians and Overseers had not paid proper attention to the affairs of the ratepayers. This laxity was a disgrace on the parties implicated, unless they came forward to clear their characters. . . . The Overseers, it appeared, employed professional gentlemen before the magistrates to get the passing of their accounts. He thought this a suspicious circumstance, and looking at the irregular keeping of the accounts referred to, it showed a gross carelessness at variance with common sense, and the good management of public or private business. These gentlemen had not done this public business as they would have done their private business! . . . (Cheers).

This was only one of a series of peculations, and they might expect more if men indifferent or incompetent were appointed to public office. . . . It was called a Poor Law, and it was a *poor* law. The Poor Officers had nothing to do but spend money, and the *poor* ratepayers to pay for it . . . (Laughter).'

Since complete silence descends on the aftermath of this notable scandal, at least so far as the Minutes of the Proceedings of the Vestry Meetings are concerned, it is impossible to tell how much of the money Benjamin Slater had embezzled was recovered by the Township. At that meeting on 22nd July it was stated that 'he had three houses and a piece of land, but they were mortgaged, and it was uncertain whether there would be any surplus. An insurance on his life for £1,000 and the proceeds of the sale of his furniture would be available but it could not be stated whether they would suffice to pay his debts'. One can understand why 'Mr Slater's executors had refused to act'.

What I should like to know is the fate of Benjamin Slater's widow and his orphan children. Was poor Ann Slater, lately the well-to-do wife of a respected public servant, left almost destitute with four young children to face the sudden and terrible disgrace which had been brought upon the family? Had Benjamin Slater contrived to leave any assets which could not be seized by the Townships and his other creditors? Had Ann known what was going on, or had she been ignorant and innocent until the blow fell?

I have so far found little definite trace of the family after 1844. At the time of the 1851 census there was apparently no Ann Slater of the right age living in Sheffield, but Charles J Slater, 20, a steel merchant's apprentice and his brother Henry B Slater, 8, a scholar, who were lodging with Mr and Mrs Rippon and their family in Fulwood Road must surely have been Benjamin's sons. Later, at the time of the 1871 census Charles Joseph Slater, 40, a steel manufacturer, lived at 11 Spring Hill in Crookesmoor with his wife Marianne and his son John B who was fifteen. If this was indeed Benjamin's son it seems that he had retrieved the family's good name and fortune.

If any of my readers are descended from him I hope that they will forgive my having unearthed this long-forgotten scandal. With hindsight it is clear that a system of local government which worked reasonably well in an eighteenth century rural area would inevitably prove quite inadequate to the demands of a rapidly growing industrial city in the nineteenth century. The professional gentlemen and manufacturers who were nominally in control as Overseers, Guardians and Surveyors were far too busy making their own money to give much attention to the public business of the Township, and were only too happy to let such an efficient servant as Benjamin Slater take more and more of the work off their hands. Small wonder that an intelligent and capable man found it all too easy to divert some of the ratepayers' funds into his own pocket, and that his employers may have preferred not to enquire too closely into his activities. Human nature was much the same in those early Victorian times as it is today!

Notice of the Vestry Meeting at which Benjamin Slater's misdeeds were first made public.

George Wostenholm

◆ Giles Robinson with additional material
by Lois Everson and Edward Oldfield

George Wostenholm was the first major developer of the
Sharrow and Nether Edge suburbs, as only piecemeal efforts
had been made in this direction before he laid out his estates
for housing. He was born in 1800, the son of an already
successful town cutler also named George. He learnt the
cutlery trade from his father who took him into partnership at
the Rockingham Works on Rockingham Street (now
demolished).

After his father's death in 1833 George was in sole
command of the family firm and he continued to develop the
company and to expand its North American trade. This trade
was the most important part of the business, and in 1836
George made the first of over thirty business trips to America
where the firm's I.XL trademark had become widely known.
The famous American frontiersman James Bowie turned to
Wostenholm when he needed a producer for his special design
of blade called the Bowie knife. One of these I.XL knives was
found on Bowie after his death at the Alamo. During the
American Civil War the firm maintained an office and a
storeroom in New York, and rumour had it that George was
involved with illegal gun-running.

The firm's success, especially in the American trade,
meant a move to larger premises in 1848. These were the
Washington Works which stood on Eldon Street and
Wellington Street. Wostenholm neither named nor built these
works but rather began to use the whole premises as one,
making it the largest works in the town at that time. He also
considerably extended the works over a period of years. A
vivid picture of life under the Wostenholm regime is given by
Henry Coward who worked at the Works as a boy but later
became a famous choir master and was knighted for services to
choral work. In his last years he lived at 6 Kenwood Road,

George Wostenholm, the Captain of Industry.

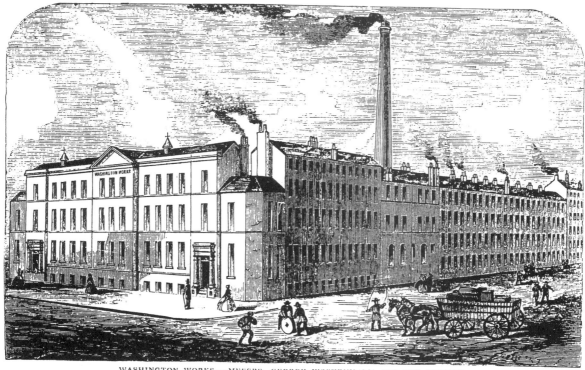

WASHINGTON WORKS.—MESSRS. GEORGE WOSTENHOLM AND SON LIMITED.

which carries a plaque to his memory. He gives a rare picture of the lives of the workmen whose skills and labours Wostenholm exploited to make a fortune and which enabled him to develop the Sharrow and Nether Edge suburbs.

Coward was born in Liverpool and when he first came to the Works at an early age, in about 1863, he had been given a more middle class upbringing than most of his fellow workers and he was nicknamed 'gentleman's boy' until he became proficient in the Sheffield dialect. At that time the building was a dirty, insanitary place with lots of busy little rooms and many passage ways and stairwells. It was a warren, but a very secure warren as George Wostenholm was extremely security conscious. All windows were barred and someone stayed on the premises at night. He was very personally involved in the running of his works and to ensure the high standards he demanded for his products he would frequently check work himself. Wostenholm inspected work by striking blades on a tiny anvil to search for defects, it was his intention to ensure sound blades in every knife the firm sold.

This testing system worked in quite an arbitrary way however. When Wostenholm was in a good mood there was a rush by the men to get work examined but 'if the old devil was on the perch' no-one went unless forced; Wostenholm's fits of anger were quite something to see, Coward tells us. Even on his death bed he had work sent to him to check. 'Georgie' as he was known in the Works, was considered a good master by the harsh standards of his day, partly because he gave out work in good quantities, unlike other masters who gave out work by the half dozen or so. Nevertheless he had many sharp practices such as binding men to serve him through loans of £5 or £10 which were often hard to pay back. He also had a rule of 'fourteen to the dozen', in other words he paid for a dozen but demanded fourteen items for that price.

It was said of George Wostenholm that his 'whole thought and ideas — apart from realising a fortune — seemed to be centred in achieving in his cutlery the legend of his trademark I. XL'. He was a workaholic, and even at Church he would sometimes be seen reading business letters during the sermon! He turned down various public offices to better pursue his business. Twice he refused to become Master Cutler because he would be in America at the time of the Feast but was persuaded to take the office in 1856. He was, however, a JP and he had various business interests outside his cutlery firm, one of which was as Chairman of Truswell's Brewery Co Ltd. However his most important non-cutlery occupation was that of property developer. He had been buying land in the vicinity of Cherry Tree Hill at Nether Edge since 1835 and on this he decided to build himself a country residence and develop a suburb. He was said to have been inspired by his visits to Kenwood near the Oneida Lake in New York State to name his own house Kenwood.

Work on the house started in 1844 and a leading Sheffield architect, William Flockton, was employed to design the house and out-buildings whilst Robert Marnock, a leading landscape gardener who had come to Sheffield to lay out the Botanical Gardens after working on Regent's Park in London planned the grounds. Flockton designed the house in the then fashionable Tudor/Gothic style which he had used a few years earlier for the Ecclesall Bierlow Union Workhouse, now Nether Edge Hospital. The house was built mainly from a limestone known as 'grey Derbyshire marble' quarried at Stanton and more usually used for making mantlepieces. As a result Kenwood was known as 'the only marble house' in the neighbourhood. Wostenholm moved into his new home in either 1845 or 1846 from his previous residence at The Mount, Broomhill, which had also been designed by Flockton.

Once his house was completed Wostenholm began to develop his property around it. Between 1851 and 1853 he laid out the roads, again employing Robert Marnock to supervise the layout and the planting of the many trees which are such a lovely feature of the area today. He left Marnock £3,000 in his will but whether this was a gift or to pay off debts is not clear. Marnock later worked on other individual gardens, for example Spring Leigh in Rundle Road, which was built in 1868

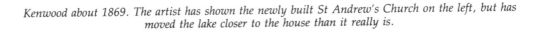

Kenwood about 1869. The artist has shown the newly built St Andrew's Church on the left, but has moved the lake closer to the house than it really is.

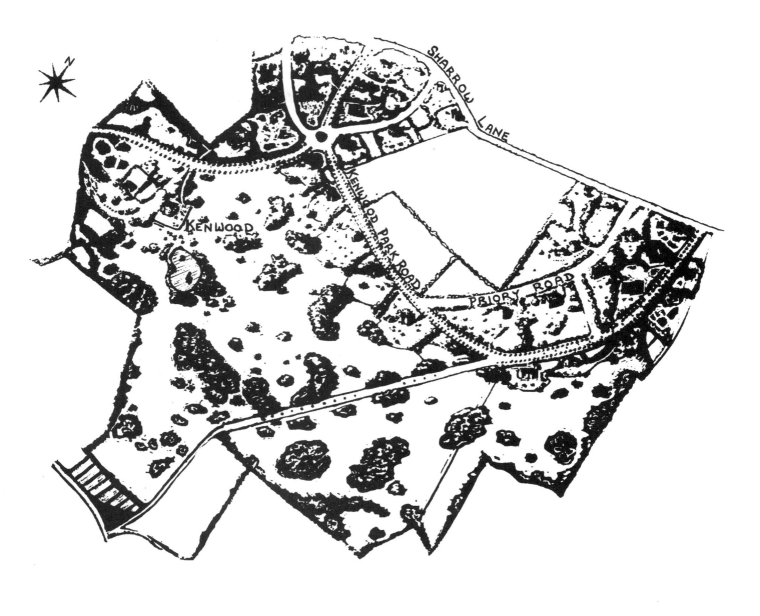

for Henry Carr Booth, another cutlery manufacturer and, further afield, he designed Weston Park and High Hazels Park.

Washington Road, named after the family works, was the first on which housing was built in 1851–53, followed by Priory Road (first houses 1851–1853), Wostenholm Road (first houses 1855) and Kenwood Park Road (first house 1861). From about 1860 to 1868 'a large number of respectable residences' were built in most of the roads. An artist's impression was drawn in 1853 of the ideal suburban development which Wostenholm would have liked, showing lots of large villas in large individual grounds. However, the reality was much more varied and only Spring Leigh and some of the houses on Kenwood Road fulfilled his ideal. In the other roads housing was generally packed more closely in rows of standardised villa residences (profit first as always!).

Wostenholm's initial development was soon being extended as Sheffield's suburban movement gathered strength. Between 1853 and 1855 the Nether Edge estate had been laid out by a land society called The Reform Freehold Land Society. This became the Montgomery Land Society in which Wostenholm was associated with Thomas Steade whose story is told elsewhere in this book. In addition to Nether Edge, Wostenholm had an interest in other speculations elsewhere in Sheffield, for example in an early attempt to develop land at Ranmoor.

Map of the Kenwood Estate showing roads laid out by 1853. Apart from Kenwood itself, most of the houses shown are fictional and intended to show prospective buyers the type of development Wostenholm hoped to promote.

As the suburb grew around his home, Wostenholm put up a second gatehouse to the estate. This was far grander than the original gate and lodge which stands at the corner of Cherry Tree Road and Kenwood Road. It faces the junction of Sharrow View, Kenwood Road, Kenwood Bank, Rundle Road and Kenwood Park Road. It was a proud advertisement of his wealth and status even bearing his new coat of arms granted in 1868. This was based on that belonging to his ancestors in the 17th century. The stone carving of this coat of arms is by Henry Hems, Wostenholm's nephew who was a sculptor and artist specialising mainly in church decor. Hems' name can just be made out below the actual carving, now nearly obliterated by having been sand blasted.

Within his little kingdom Wostenholm was able to entertain his many guests on a grand scale and to house his collection of paintings and other works of art. Some of this art reflected his American interests and included a painting of the

23

American Indian Princess Pocahontas. He had once tried, unsuccessfully, to buy a portrait of George Washington to add to the collection. His life style at Kenwood is indicated by the census of 1871 which shows his house to contain:

George Wostenholm, merchant, manufacturer of cutlery and JP, employing 388 men, 83 boys, 54 girls and women; Eliza Maria Wostenholm, aged 30, his wife, of Gosport, Hampshire, and Ann Moncrieffe Rundle, 23, Eliza Maria's sister, also born at Gosport. Servants in the house are listed as — lady's maid, cook, upper housemaid, under housemaid and footman. Living in the lodge were the head gardener and his wife. In the stable — the coachman and his wife and two children with two gardeners as lodgers.

Wostenholm was married three times and each of his wives lived at Kenwood. His first wife was Mary Hobson who had been his school teacher. She died in 1853 and he then married Frances Crookes, daughter of a London merchant, who died in 1865. His third wife was Eliza Maria Rundle. Eliza and her sister are shown in the 1871 census above; their names are commemorated in Rundle and Moncrieffe Roads. Among the visitors entertained at Kenwood was the Sheffield poet James Montgomery who had been Wostenholm's friend and neighbour at The Mount. Not long before his death Montgomery planted two trees in the grounds for Mrs Wostenholm and presented her with a poem about the occasion.

Wostenholm made many acts of charity during his lifetime, something of an obligation for the Victorian middle class. He gave towards various religious buildings including a vicarage for St Mary's Church, now 17 Kenwood Park Road, built in 1862–4. He was a benefactor of his local church, St Andrew's, which contains a stained glass window in memory of his first two wives. However, like many Victorians, his charity was somewhat hypocritical or as his workmen at the Washington Works expressed it '£100 to the missionaries and dock the workmen'.

After a year of 'very indifferent health' George Wostenholm died on 18th August 1876 leaving a fortune of over £250,000. His obituary noted that 'it would certainly have conduced more to his comfort and might probably have prolonged his day if he had in his late years devoted less thought and time to business, but it was not in the nature of Mr Wostenholm to do so'. At his funeral on the 22nd August among the thousand or so onlookers were many of the most important figures of Sheffield including members of the Mappin, Wake, Rodgers and Jessop families together with Sir John Brown who had been a near neighbour at Shirle Hill till 1865. Also at the funeral were Robert Marnock, Thomas Steade and Henry Carr Booth of Spring Leigh, Rundle Road. He was buried at Ecclesall Church where his grave and monument still stand. It is also a memorial to his third wife, Eliza Maria. After her husband's death Eliza gave land for a Wostenholm

A croquet party at Kenwood towards the end of George Wostenholm's life. He stands behind the table, with his wife Eliza sitting on his right and her sister Miss Rundle standing on his left.

Memorial Hall and she defrayed the cost of £11,000. This hall used to stand on Queen Street near the Cathedral. Eliza later married a Thomas E Beaumont with whom she lived at Kenwood until she died in 1886, aged 45. After Thomas Beaumont's death the estate came to Eliza's unmarried sister Annie Moncrieffe Rundle. She did not die until 1922 and older residents of Nether Edge remember her being driven round the district in her horse-drawn carriage. Two years after her death the house and part of the grounds were sold to the Sheffield Refreshment Houses organisation and for many years it was a temperance hotel and, in the same decade, housing was built on the roads bordering the estate.

Wostenholm left no children and, after his death, his cutlery company was never quite the same. The twentieth century has been a devastating time for Sheffield's cutlery industry as a result of foreign competition and Wostenholm's have been one of the casualties.

The firm finished at 'old' Washington Works in 1972 and the trade name and trade mark I*XL were taken over and incorporated with Joseph Rodgers & Sons Ltd as Rodgers Wostenholm in 1973. For a while they operated from a factory at Heeley until this was closed and demolished. A 'new' Washington Works has been established at Allen Street where products still bearing the Rodgers and Wostenholm trade marks continue to be made and exported to many countries.

The 'old' Washington Works were demolished in 1978 but the Washington pub nearby saved part of the stone name tablet to use as a name on their building where it can be seen on the Wellington Street side.

John Rodgers

◆ Giles Robinson

John Rodgers, painted by the local artist Richard Smith.

The most famous cutlery firm in Sheffield's history was that of Joseph Rodgers and Sons. The man chiefly responsible for that success was John Rodgers, a son of Joseph Rodgers, the founder. He was a brilliant business man and devoted his life to the company. He built upon the foundations his father had laid to make his company world famous. A visit to the works of Joseph Rodgers and Sons, especially to their showrooms with the finest and most skilled pieces of workmanship, became a must for distinguished visitors to Sheffield, including royalty.

John Rodgers followed the movement of other town manufacturers who were building country residences in the Abbeydale, Sharrow and Nether Edge area. In this he joined James Wilson, the builder of Brinkcliffe Towers, John Shortridge, the builder of Chippinghouse and the better known George Wostenholm of Kenwood, all of whom are dealt with elsewhere in this book. He built his house 'regardless of expense' and called it Abbeydale House. It was built of polished Anston stone in the Italian style to the design of a little known Sheffield architect, William Rooke-Harrison and he moved there from his old home, Hillsborough Hall, in 1850. At that time Abbeydale House and Kenwood were the largest country residences on this side of Sheffield and their owners' example served to increase the demand for this kind of residence and, in turn, for more affordable suburban dwellings.

Like George Wostenholm, John Rodgers had begun acquiring land in the area during the 1830s and, by the time of his death in 1850, had amassed a considerable estate including land at Millhouses, Norton Hammer, Archer Lane and what became the Archer Road area. Unlike Wostenholm he showed no interest in developing his property for housing but like Wostenholm he avoided public life in order to devote his

energies to his business. Together he and Wostenholm were the most important cutlery manufacturers in 19th century Sheffield and, fittingly, their graves lie close together in Ecclesall churchyard.

Most of the Abbeydale House estate was sold in 1860, after John Rodgers' death, to John Firth of Thomas Firth and Sons, the great steel-making company. He built himself a house on part of the estate on the site of a farm called Holt House, the history of which goes back to medieval times. He was a trained architect and the house was built to his own design. The house still stands as an adult education centre just above Holt House Infant School with an ornamental gateway at the Abbeydale Road end of Bannerdale Road. Ater his death his executors were responsible for developing much of the estate, laying out Bannerdale Road, Carterknowle Road and part of Woodseats Road together with various other roads in the vicinity about 1900.

Abbeydale House and its gardens stayed in the Rodgers family for a while after John Rodgers' death, eventually being sold in 1896 for housing development of Barmouth, Falmouth, Plymouth and Lynmouth Roads. Most of this housing was built by Robert Hunt, a local builder, between 1896 and 1903. Abbeydale House was used as offices by the Snowite Laundry for a large part of this century and then was left derelict for a long time. In 1974 the once grand interior was a sad sight with the fine sweeping staircase leading up to a huge puddle about six inches deep on the landing. Since then the roof has been repaired and the house is now used as an antiques warehouse, but it is still a very melancholy relic of the great days of Sheffield's cutlery manufacturers.

Just up Abbeydale Road from Abbeydale House is another link with the Rodgers' firm, the villa called Abbeydale Grange, now part of the school of that name. This was built for Robert Newbold, John Rodgers' nephew and successor in the family firm. His family came to Sheffield from Coventry and Robert moved into his newly built house, from a residence in Beauchief, about 1858. He left Abbeydale Grange in the 1870s to live in the then fashionable West Retford and died in 1896. Joseph Rodgers knives, marked with the famous 'Star & Cross' trademark, are still exported to many countries where they are in demand and have a high reputation. Both Rodgers and Wostenholm are members of the Egginton Group of Companies.

Abbeydale House in 1896, before the grounds were sold for development.

Thomas Steade ◆ Giles Robinson

Born in 1821, Thomas Steade was the son of Joseph Steade of Steade and Allen, Sheffield ironfounders. Thomas joined his father in the family business at the Albion Foundry, Eyre Street, casting stove grates and kitchen ranges amongst other things. In about 1858 Thomas set up a foundry in Cemetery Road on his own, starting with a capital of £4,000. This new enterprise was probably established to specialise in iron work for his increasing building operations. He started speculative building in Cemetery Road in the 1850s and from then on he became deeply involved in property development.

Steade became associated with George Wostenholm's local developments in Nether Edge. Housing known to have been built by him includes much of the east side of Montgomery Road from Moncrieffe Road to Steade Road and many of the houses on the odd numbered side of Kenwood Park Road. In 1863 he bought land for development from George Wostenholm on which he built Crescent Road and Steade Road. From 1867 to 1883 he developed Albany, St Ronan's, Frederick, Arthur, Avenue and Belper Roads; Frederick Road and Arthur Road being named after members of his family. Other houses built by Steade include nearly all those in Chippinghouse Road from Abbeydale Road to Crescent Road. However the road itself appears to have been laid out earlier by John Shortridge and to have originally been called Shortridge Road. Shortridge was the builder of the house called Chippinghouse (see article on Shortridge).

A distinguishing feature of Steade's houses is the cast iron fixtures which he used. The most frequent iron fitting is a window lintel in the shape of a simple classical pediment although one or two are more ornamental, for example 23 Kenwood Park Road. He also used cast iron banisters, for example in 23 Montgomery Road, cast iron gateposts, for example 37 Crescent Road, and most of his houses had cast iron railings. All these would have been made in his own foundry and were also bought by other builders. One of those other builders was Francis Smith and, about 1870, he used Steade's lintels in 7 Oakdale Road and 22 Brincliffe Edge Road, for example.

Steade got involved with the Montgomery Land Society, with considerable profit. George Wostenholm is said to have conveyed land to Steade who immediately conveyed it to the Montgomery Land Society for almost double what he had paid for it, leaving him with a profit of about £6,400. Not all his plans for the development of other parts of Nether Edge and Sharrow came to fruition. He had planned to build on the Brincliffe Park estate — Chelsea, Lyndhurst, Cavendish and part of Osborne Road — but only built 18 Chelsea Road; nor did he build in Rundle Road as he had planned. One of the differences between Steade's developments and those of George Wostenholm was in the planting of trees. Wostenholm employed Robert Marnock, the landscape gardener who had laid out his own grounds at Kenwood, to plant trees on his roads but the trees on Steade's roads were less skillfully planted and too close together, and many were dead or dying by 1883. Another of Steade's local enterprises was an omnibus service. However, after competing for a time with the cheaper tramways he was ousted by them to his cost.

Apart from his developments in Nether Edge and Sharrow, Steade was involved in the Meersbrook Land Society and the Hallamshire Benefit Buidling Society. He acquired estates at Eckington, Whittington, Rawmarsh, Killamarsh, Kimberworth, Dore Moor and other districts. In Attercliffe, where Steade was involved in road making and building and also had an earthenware works, he named one of his roads Steadfast Street. That name was ill chosen for in 1888 his run of good fortune ended. Most of his enterprises had been carried out on borrowed money and in this year his creditors finally foreclosed. His business liabilities were said to be over £100,000. 'The bankrupt's mode of transacting his business has been extraordinary as he informs me no books have been kept' wrote a journalist at the time. Various complaints had already been made about Steade's practices such as building without proper drainage. The stresses of his business life and bankruptcy led to a fatal heart attack in 1889.

A Steade house, 45 Kenwood Park Road, in the 1890s when the motor car had not yet displaced the horse (see foreground).
Note the superb iron gate and railings.

The Boot Family
of Heeley and Nether Edge

◆ Shirley Meek and
Joyce Jenkinson

The firm of Henry Boot and Sons plc is nationally famous for its civil engineering and construction work. Most local people know its headquarters at Banner Cross Hall; few know that when the firm moved to its Ecclesall home in 1932 it was returning to a part of Sheffield where the Boot family had lived and worked for generations.

The Boots originally came from Middle Heeley, where they owned a farm. The farmhouse stood near the Shakespeare Inn at the top of Well Road, and its 28 acres of land stretched from Heeley Green down to the River Sheaf. Henry Boot, born in 1761, was living there at the close of the eighteenth century when Heeley was still a village two miles walk across the fields from Sheffield town. Henry had five sons named William, John, Charles, Joseph and Henry. William, the eldest, inherited the family farm. He was also a stonemason, a trade which occupied most of the male Boots for several generations, as well as a shopkeeper. By 1851, when he was 57, he was employing eight men and he and his wife, Mary, had two house servants living in, so it seems that he was quite a prosperous man.

John was in the other trade favoured by the Boots. He is said to have kept the Blackamoor Head Inn at Troway and a Samuel Boot, who was probably his son, was listed in the 1865 directory as a beer retailer and stonemason at Eckington.

The next two sons, Charles and Joseph, moved across the Sheaf valley to live near the old village of Cherry Tree Hill. By 1837 they were working together as stonemasons and builders and it seems likely that one of their first undertakings was to build the group of stone cottages at Edge Bank above Machon Bank Road. In one of these Charles was to live for the rest of his life with his wife Sarah, and to bring up his eight children. The land for the new Ecclesall Union Workhouse was bought by the Guardians of the Poor in 1839 only a few hundred yards away and building work started there in 1841.

Henry Boot in 1901, when he was running the Oxford Saw Mills and Machine Joinery Works and commanded 'the esteem and respect of his fellow-townsmen as a God-fearing, conscientious man of business'.

In 1840 the Boots built the Union Inn and the two stone houses on either side of it. The inn stood on the corner of Machon Bank Road, the old lane which linked Cherry Tree Hill with the hamlet of Machon Bank, and the new Union Road which led to the Workhouse entrance. There were obviously going to be a lot of thirsty building workers when William Flockton's fine and imposing edifice was started, and Joseph Boot was well placed in his new home to cater for them. For the next 30 years he combined the trades of publican and stonemason, and as he also owned a quarry it is possible that he and his brother Charles provided stone for the workhouse as well as beer for its builders.

Joseph and his wife Annis already had four children when they moved into the Union Inn and they went on to have three more who lived to grow up. In 1851 there were fifteen Boot children all living on Machon Bank Road, from Charles'

Houses at Edge Bank. The right hand side is little altered from the days when Charles Boot and his family lived there.

eldest, 17 year old Charles, to is youngest, 1 year old Arthur, and from Joseph's 15 year old John Henry to 1 year old Emily. It must have been noisy! But there were plenty of cousins for them all to play with, so they probably kept each other amused.

By 1871 Joseph had given up the licence of the inn, although he was still trading as a builder, and had moved next door to 11 Union Road on the corner of Osborne Road. (This was the new, more up-market name of what was originally called Workhouse Lane.) He died in 1880 but his second son, Thomas Alfred, followed him in the building trade and continued to live close by at 31 Union Road with his unmarried sister Mary Annis for many years.

Cabman waiting for custom outside the Union Hotel, a little after Joseph Boot's time as landlord.

Charles Boot retired early from the stonemason business when he was only in his mid-fifties, and he died in 1867 aged 62. His widow Sarah continued to live at Edge Bank, and in 1871 her daughters Fanny and Elizabeth and her youngest son Arthur were still living at home. By this time they were calling themselves Boote with an 'e', though two other daughters, Sarah and Ellen, who were both Board School mistresses, obviously thought nothing of this genteelism and in their 1879 directory entries stick to plain old-fashioned Boot.

Not to be outdone, by 1876 Mr Joseph Boote, the retired publican, had also acquired an 'e'!

Young Arthur Boote founded the firm of Boote and Rhodes, ornamental engravers, of 52 High Street, and by 1883 he was living in a very large house at 12 Victoria Road, Broomhall. His elder brother Charles, a commercial traveller, remained faithful to Boot without an 'e' and continued to live in Nether Edge at 24 Rupert Road.

Joseph's younger brother Henry and his wife Eliza were staying with him at the Union Inn on census day in 1851. Perhaps they were learning the licensing trade, for in 1856 Henry was keeping the Britannia public house in Portobello Street.

Over in Heeley, in the meantime, William Boot's two sons, William and Charles, had grown up and married. William, the elder, was a stonemason and shopkeeper in New George Street until his father's death. Charles, the younger, lived next door to his parents' farm. His trade is given as 'stonemason' in the 1851 census return, but he must also have been helping his father since his occupation was given as 'farmer' when his elder children were baptised at Heeley Church.

On his father's death William moved back to Heeley, and at the time of the 1861 census the two brothers were living next door to each other in Boot's Yard while their widowed mother, with a servant, was still in the old family home. The 1863 directory lists William and Charles Boot as 'stonemasons and quarry owners, of Heeley and Brincliffe Edge' but by October 1864 William Boot was announcing to patrons that he was starting business on his own. This cannot have been successful because shortly afterwards he was declared bankrupt, though he was discharged from bankruptcy in March 1865. Troubles came thick and fast for the family. Later that year they lost a two month old baby, and in May 1866 William Boot died at the early age of 42. He was buried at St Mary's, Bramall Lane, and his widow Ann was left to bring up a family of five. She moved to Highfields, where she lived for many years.

What had happened to cause the rift between William and Charles? Family tradition says that the break came when Charles went off with the cart and other equipment for the building business while William was ill, and Ann blamed this trouble for William's early death.

One of the Triumphal Arches erected to welcome Queen Victoria to Sheffield in 1897, several of which were built by Henry Boot's firm.

Whatever the truth may have been, the land and farm were sold. Work had begun on the new Sheffield to Chesterfield railway in 1865, and this line passed over part of the Boot property. In 1871 Oak Street Methodist Church was built on the land where the farm stood, and later a barn which had been attached to the farmhouse was converted into a lecture hall for the church.

By the time of the 1871 census Charles Boot and his family were living in Pearl Street, Sharrow, and he was working as a corn miller; perhaps this was at the old Broomhall Corn Mill which stood on the river Porter at the bottom of Ecclesall Road. His second son Arthur was following the family trade of mason, but his eldest son Henry was an apprentice joiner. At this point in time their more affluent Boote cousins in Edge Bank and Union Road must have thought of Charles and his family as poor relations, but it was young Henry Boot who was to make their name famous — without an 'e'.

After the usual seven years' apprenticeship Henry worked as a joiner for several Sheffield building firms before setting up his own business in 1886 at the age of 35. He bought the Oxford Saw Mills and was soon building large private houses, public houses and later new 'picture houses'. His sons Charles and Edward both joined him in the business at an early age and several of the elaborate Triumphal Arches erected for Queen Victoria's visit to Sheffield in 1897 were the work of the firm of Henry Boot and Sons. They also built the Applied Science Building on Mappin Street for Sheffield University in 1902.

The firm's fortunes were really made during the First World War when Henry Boot and Sons carried out many large Government construction contracts, notably the Army Camp at Catterick in Yorkshire, Manston Aerodrome in Kent and Calshot Seaplane Base near Southampton. They are said to have owed their start on this work to a chance encounter; Charles Boot, on his way to York, stopped to give a lift to a Government official whose car had broken down. Following their conversation the Boot firm was given a contract for building Army huts, and never looked back. After the war they went on to increasingly large projects all over the world which were to make the firm internationally famous.

Henry Boot's son Charles followed his father as Chairman in 1921. Born to a humble home in Ellin Street, he later lived in considerable splendour at Sugworth Hall near Strines and then in the still more imposing Thornbridge Hall near Ashford in the Water. When the firm moved its headquarters to Banner Cross in 1932 he must have looked out at the now disused quarries on Brincliffe Edge where his grandfather and great uncle had worked seventy years earlier, and reflected with pride on the growth of the family business.

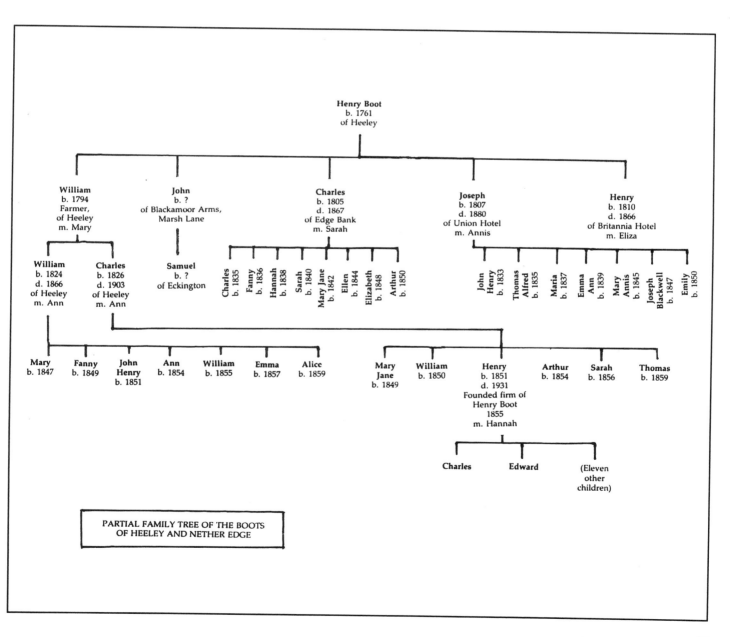

PARTIAL FAMILY TREE OF THE BOOTS
OF HEELEY AND NETHER EDGE

Sir John Brown at Shirle Hill

◆ Joan Flett

Sir John Brown.

Imagine the Prime Minister visiting a house in Nether Edge in 1988; imagine the fuss; imagine the security precautions! In 1862 the Prime Minister of the day, Lord Palmerston, visited John Brown at his home, Shirle Hill, apparently with remarkably little fuss. Lord Palmerston was in Sheffield to attend a civic banquet given by John during his second year as Mayor and to visit the Atlas Works of J Brown & Co to witness the manufacture of the enormous sheets of armour plating used for warships. By 1867 three-quarters of the British Navy ships were armoured with plates rolled at the works.

John Brown was born on 6th December 1816, in Flavell's Yard, Fargate. At that time this was a good class residential area and John's father was a slater and builder of reasonably good standing. John went to a small school held in a garret and there he met his future wife, Mary Schofield, the daughter of a local auctioneer. John left school at fourteen and, despite his father's wish that he become a draper, insisted that he wanted to become a 'merchant'. His father agreed to apprentice him to a firm of general traders. For the first two years John received no wages and then six shillings a week. When his time expired his father gave him a sovereign and a suit of clothes.

In 1836 this firm changed to manufacturing files and cutlery and when John was twenty-one he was offered a share in the business. However, his father and an uncle guaranteed £500 for him to set up in business on his own. He started in Orchard Street as a manufacturer of cutlery and joiner's tools and in 1848 moved to new premises in Furnival Street. This was the era of rapid expansion in the railways and in those early days there was no system of shock absorption and carriages were simply joined together by long chains. John invented a conical steel buffer which was widely adopted. By 1850 over 150 sets a week were being made. This success was

Ball at the Cutlers' Hall, Sheffield, to celebrate the completion of Mr Brown's two years' mayoralty.

the foundation of John's future prosperity and he later incorporated a buffer into his coat of arms.

The business continued to expand using several sites until, in 1854, John bought the Queen's Works on Saville Street. This was a three acre site and production started with 200 workers on 1st January 1856, at the renamed Atlas Works. It was later stated poetically that, at that time, 'there was scarcely anything to indicate that in a few short years the country for miles would be desolated by the smoke fiend. From the window of his counting house Sir John Brown looked upon the wild hyacinths waving their plumes amid the shadow of pleasant trees'. Within three years chimneys covered the site with smoke and by 1867 the works extended to twenty-one acres!

John married Mary Schofield in 1839 and until 1865 they resided at Shirle Hill. The sale plans of 1865 show that they also owned a considerable amount of adjoining property including two other houses on Cherry Tree Road and one on Williamson Road. Shirle Hill had 'pleasure grounds tastefully laid out and containing the choicest shrubs and evergreens' and there were potting sheds, a peach house, a vinery, pine pits (for the cultivation of pineapples) and a loose box for two horses.

During his residence at Shirle Hill John was twice Mayor of Sheffield, in 1861 and 1862, and Master Cutler in 1865. He also held the latter office again in 1866. It was in his second year of office as Mayor that he held the first civic banquet given by a mayor. Lord Palmerston accepted an invitation to attend only the day before the banquet so that preparations to receive him were hurried. On the morning of his arrival, on Friday 8th August 1862, members of the Town Council met at the new Victoria Hotel and then moved to the platform at the Victoria Station to greet the Prime Minister. Barriers had been put up to keep onlookers back and a strong body of police was on duty. One of them made the ludicrous mistake of taking the Mayor by the collar and telling him to be about his business! When the seventy-eight year old Prime Minister arrived the crowd surged forward and a group of grinders in their work-day clothes shook his hand and one man cried out, 'God bless thee, lad'. He was driven to Shirle Hill and apart from 'welcome' banners in the Town centre there was no demonstration. At the reception before the banquet in the Cutlers' Hall he cracked jokes with the guests and there was continuous laughter. The meal had been prepared by the manager of the Victoria Hotel and included turtle soup followed by seven different fish dishes, sixteen entrées and various desserts accompanied by ten wines. After 'the cloths were drawn' the ladies were admitted to the 'orchestra' and were served dessert.

The Prime Minister returned to Shirle Hill that night and next morning held a breakfast meeting with various local worthies. He expressed 'his admiration of the delightful scenery which the Mayor's residence commands' and John offered to drive him out to see more scenery. They drove up to Brincliffe Edge and then to the Botanical Gardens before proceeding to the Atlas Works where the various production processes were inspected.

As they left the works they passed the 'cottages' of the workers. Many had their doors open and Lord Palmerston commented on the cleanliness of many of them, on how neatly they were prepared and that most of them had a comfortable sofa. He asked particularly about the accommodation and was told that they had a cellar, two bedrooms and a living room. He returned to Shirle Hill for lunch and then left for the station. As he passed down Cemetery Road there were cheering crowds and he shook hands with many people. At the station the crowd struggled to get near him and in his carriage he was besieged by people wanting to shake his hand. The local newspaper reporter wrote 'it must have been a relief to him when the train started'.

Another indication of the social life of the Town at that time is given by the description of the two soirées held at the Cutlers' Hall after the completion of John's two years as Mayor. The *Illustrated London News* of 21st November 1863, reported that the elite of the society of the Town and County attended. They arrived at eight o'clock and promenaded, chatted and listened to music. At twelve o'clock 'a most recherché supper' was served. A prominent feature of the decorations was a portrait of John presented to the Town by the townspeople. The large mirrors round the hall were draped with richly embroidered white lace and festooned with artificial flowers and the arched roof over the orchestra was also draped with lace backed by delicate mauve material. The *News* went on to state that during the previous eighteen months John had been visited at Shirle Hill by Lord Palmerston, the Lords of the Admiralty (who had also inspected the rolling of armour plating) and all the 'neighbouring nobility'. It continued to describe his munificence to all religious denominations and charities during his years of office as almost unlimited. On the occasion of the marriage of the Prince of Wales his liberality had been great, 'No town in England put on a gayer appearance . . .'

In 1865 John sold Shirle Hill and moved to Endcliffe Hall on which he spent nearly £150,000 and he was knighted in 1876. Although he had moved out of Nether Edge he continued his local connection as Chairman of the Ecclesall Bierlow Board of Guardians, which administered the Workhouse on Union Road, for twenty years from 1873 until he moved away from Sheffield.

During his later years John's business dealings were not so successful, profits sank and eventually he resigned through ill health with a payment of £200,000 for the goodwill and the prestigious name of the company. His wife died in 1881 and they had no children. He suffered increasing illness and took little part in public life. He usually spent the winters in the south of England, eventually leaving Sheffield in 1892. He died a year later on 17th December at the home of friends in Kent. He was buried at Ecclesall Church beside his wife.

Shirle Hill in 1865.

Thomas Jessop

◆ Irene Clegg

Mr Thomas Jessop.

Thomas Jessop was the son of William Jessop the founder of William Jessop & Sons, Steel Manufacturers, and in 1862 was living at Sharrow House, Sharrow Lane. This house no longer exists but it stood roughly opposite to what was for many years the Welfare of the Blind Workshops.

He was a well known figure in the town. In 1843 he became a member of the first Town Council and by 1863 was Master Cutler and Mayor in the same year — a feat which has not been repeated since. After the Sheffield Flood in 1864 he was responsible for raising all the cash for the relief of families affected by the flood.

On 12th December 1863, due to the efforts of a Dr James Aveling, a lecturer in the Medical School, a public meeting was held in the Cutlers' Hall, chaired by Thomas Jessop, to promote the establishment of a Lying-in Hospital for Women and by June 1864 a house in Figtree Lane had been secured at a rental of £60 pa and equipped with six beds. This building is now occupied by Cleggs, the solicitors, and a commemorative plaque has been placed on the wall. It is interesting that originally there existed much prejudice against the establishment of a Hospital for Women in Sheffield and that it was not founded without considerable difficulty.

Accommodation eventually proved inadequate and in 1874 Mr Jessop announced his intention to provide a new building. The cost of building was £17,000. Equipment, land purchase and furnishings brought the total to over £30,000, all of which was met by this Victorian philanthropist. He later left Sharrow House and by 1876 was living at Endcliffe Grange where he died in 1887, but it is a nice thought that one of our local residents was the founder of the Jessop Hospital for Women which became internationally respected.

One of his grandsons (a Trustee of the Jessop Hospital) gave a short address to the final meeting of the Hospital Committee a few days before the start of the National Health Service in 1948, in which he recalled being taken as a small boy to visit his grandfather. He remembered Thomas Jessop sitting in a chair with a silver-mounted spittoon by his side. This was operated by a foot pedal which opened the lid when required and then closed it with a clang! "What wouldn't I have given for half an hour alone with that wonderful contraption", he said with great feeling.

The Sheffield Hospital for Women, Figtree Lane, Sheffield. Opened in 1864 with six beds.

The Smiths

A Local Family of Artists
◆ Giles Robinson

The three artists of the Smith family were all well known to the Sheffield of their day. The brothers Edwin and Richard and Edwin's son Theophilus typify the provincial Victorian artists of their period.

Edwin Smith (1810–1889) came from an old Sheffield family. His father James was an engraver, and so was perhaps more inclined to encourage his sons in artictic careers. Edwin commenced business as a sculptor, designer and modeller in Devonshire Street about 1840. His works can still be found all around Sheffield, mostly in churches and graveyards; the Chantrey monument and grave at Norton is perhaps the most famous of them. Although Edwin Smith carried out much ordinary tombwork there were also more unusual pieces such as the imposing monument with a full-length relief portrait in the General Cemetery to George Bennet, missionary and friend to Montgomery, the poet. (Like many other graves in the cemetery this has recently attracted the attention of vandals.)

Between 1847 and 1851 Edwin set up the Cemetery Road Marble and Stone Works close to the old Broomhall corn mill which was still powered by the River Porter. When they first opened the works were on the outskirts of Sheffield close to open countryside, and Cemetery Road had not yet been built up. The site was convenient for the General Cemetery, however, where Edwin had a good trade. Now it lies underneath the Sheffield and Ecclesall Co-operative stores, themselves soon to be demolished. Like so many Victorians Edwin busied himself with a variety of different occupations. He took death masks, sold scale models of Jerusalem in its landscape setting and hired out water beds for fever patients!

Edwin Smith posed with some of his works for a newspaper photograph.

Theophilus' mother and his sister Priscilla.

In 1852 he bought land in Nether Edge and started to build himself a house on what was to become Edgebrook Road. The land had been part of the Bright estate. The Bright family was of high standing in eighteenth century Sheffield, and had owned both the Nether Edge farm (now the Brincliffe Oaks Hotel) and the Upper Edge farm, which stood roughly where the Fountside flats have been built between Oakdale and Edgebrook Roads. In the 1840s the land was owned by John Bright, who was living in Leicestershire. He attempted to develop his Upper Edge estate for housing, but at that time there was not much interest in moving out to this new suburb. Audrey Cottage was built as a pair of semi-detached villas in 1845 on the corner of the recently laid out Edgebrook and Union Roads to the design of William Flockton, the architect of the newly completed Ecclesall Union Workhouse which stood close by.

No further houses were built in this part of Nether Edge until 1853, when Edwin Smith built Edgebrook Cottage (now 6 Edgebrook Road) on the plot of land next to Audrey Cottage. Over the imposing stone fireplace in the kitchen are carved his initials, the date and the motto 'Waste not, want not'. This fine piece of craftsmanship may well have been carved by Edwin himself. At Edgebrook Cottage he lived with his wife Mary, his son Theophilus and his daughter Priscilla for many years.

In 1857 his brother Richard (1818–1890) came to live close by. Richard was a portrait painter and commercial artist whose talents had enabled him to have his first exhibit in the Royal Academy when he was only twenty. He later painted many of Sheffield's most famous inhabitants, including both Sir John Brown, the great steel maker who lived for a time at Shirle Hill on Cherry Tree Road, and William Bragge, the managing director of John Brown and Co, who followed his employer as the owner of Shirle Hill. Richard Smith also painted John Rodgers, the cutler and builder of Abbeydale House, and Thomas Rawson Barker who lived at The Edge on Ladysmith Avenue. He was the youngest man ever to be Mayor of Sheffield, and his name is commemorated in Barkers Road.

Mrs Edwin Smith reading on the terrace at Edgebrook Cottage, taken by Theophilus about 1875.

Richard Smith moved to Nether Edge from an old house called Broadfield in Broadfield Road. The large house which he built in 1857 still stands on Union Road opposite the top of Oakdale Road, though it has since been divided into two and is now nos. 94 and 96 Union Road.

Theophilus Smith at work on a bust in his studio.

Edwin's son Theophilus (1838–1886) was trained as an artist, and there still exists a notebook he kept in his teens containing theories of portrait painting, notes on the use of colour and other points useful to a working artist. Like his father he also worked as a sculptor, designer and modeller. He made busts and medallions of such Victorian worthies as Dickens, Carlyle the historian, Titus Salt the Bradford textile magnate and Robert Hadfield, founder of Hadfields steel company. He also did various pieces of two-dimensional design work such as illuminated addresses. Theophilus Smith is best known, however, as one of Sheffield's pioneer photographers. In his two illustrated books 'Wharncliffe, Wortley and the Valley of the Don' and 'Sheffield and Neighbourhood' he left to posterity some of the most important early photographs of this area which exist. The photographs in these books are all hand printed and have been glued in by hand. He also took an excellent series of photographs after the great Sheffield flood of 1864, recording the trail of devastation left behind as the waters of the broken Dale Dyke dam swept down the Loxley Valley and through the heart of the town. For a time he was a commercial photographer, taking 'carte de visite' portraits of local people.

After Theophilus Smith had married and started a family he went, in 1869, to live at 21 Cherry Tree Road, then known as Shirle Hill Cottage but now called Lamorna. He seems to have taken over the direction of the Cemetery Road works from his father, for in the 1871 census Theophilus' occupation is given as 'sculptor, employing 17 men, 12 boys and 1 girl. Ornamental marble, stone and metal worker'. In 1874 he built himself a house at the corner of Oakdale and Adelaide Road, no 25 Oakdale Road, and moved there with his wife Louisa Caroline, his daughters Etheldreda Louisa and Ellen Gwyneth who were eight and five years old, and his son Edwin who was three. The gardens of his father's house swept down to where the little Edge Brook ran under rustic bridges, and then up to Oakhill Road opposite no 25. It must have been a lovely place for small children to play, and there Theophilus took an enchanting series of photographs of his father and mother, his sister Priscilla and his own three children.

Edwin Smith did not stay much longer at Edgebrook Cottage, however. In 1876 he sold it and moved into a far smaller house at 10 Byron Road. His brother Richard's fortunes also seem to have waned, since about the same time he too moved out of his large house into a semi-detached one at 24 Byron Road, though later he did move again into the bigger house next door at no 26.

Edwin's last years must have been sad, since he outlived two of his grandchildren and also his son. In 1881 small Edwin died, aged ten, and in 1885 the Smiths lost Ellen Gwyneth at the age of sixteen. Finally in 1886 Theophilus died, aged forty-eight. A near-contemporary account of his life says that 'he brought on an early death for himself as a result of injudicious habits', but leaves us to guess what they were. Did he take to drink? Was it grief for the loss of his son and daughter, perhaps added to financial troubles with the family business, which drove him to an early end?

He lies buried with young Edwin and Ellen in Ecclesall churchyard, in a family grave whose tombstone also records the burials of his wife and his daughter Etheldreda in 1923. The photographs which Theophilus Smith left behind, however, are a far more vivid memorial than any gravestone to his family and to the Sheffield they knew.

Edwin Smith standing by his garden gate at Edgebrook Cottage.

Young Edwin and Ellen, taken by their father in the Edgebrook Cottage garden.

James Montgomery
Poet, Journalist, Editor, Hymn Writer ◆ Malcolm Weston

James Montgomery as a young man.

James Montgomery and the notorious Charles Peace have little in common except that both are strongly associated with the district and yet neither actually lived here.

Montgomery Road, the Montgomery Oaks, Montgomery College (the small, chapel-like building at the top of Cemetery Road) were all named after him as was the much more recent Montgomery Hall in Norfolk Street.

Born of Irish missionary parents in 1771 he received a classical education at the Moravian Brotherhood School at Calverley (Leeds) and came to Sheffield as a counting office clerk for Joseph Gales, the proprietor of the Sheffield Register — a small weekly newspaper with extreme political opinions.

When Gales was obliged to leave as a consequence of his political views in 1794 Montgomery carried on the business and changed the title to the 'Sheffield Iris' under which name the paper flourished for many years and became the forerunner of the present Sheffield Newspapers Ltd.

The business was conducted at Hartshead, Montgomery living 'over the shop' for many years until he rented an apartment at The Mount, Broomhill, as a residence more suitable for a man of letters.

At that period, newspapers were less concerned with actual news and more interested in the dissemination of philosophical and scientific opinion. This led Montgomery to

One of the fine oak trees known as the 'Montgomery Oak' which stood on the corner of Oakhill Road and Oakdale Road.

seek out and form lifetime friendships with local men of some standing in order to find material for his columns. He was no great writer himself (other than his poems and hymns) but could ably convey the views of others.

Although a gentle, shy and non-combative man he had an impish and gleeful sense of humour. He and several other notable personalities of the town used to meet weekly in the Bull Inn, Wicker, to talk over affairs of the moment and they hatched a hoax against the then Mayor of Doncaster who had offended them in some way. They arranged for a letter — purporting to come from the King — to be delivered to the Mayor offering a Knighthood and bidding him to come to London to receive it. The Mayor took this fake letter seriously and he and his wife prepared for the journey to London. Only on the eve of his departure did he think to lay the matter before the Corporation, when the hoax (but not the hoaxers) was discovered. The following week a highly satirical poem about the whole affair appeared in the 'Iris' to add to the Mayor's discomfiture.

It seems that Montgomery was the sort of amiable and interesting man to whom no doors were closed. He was a great friend of Samuel Roberts, Chantrey the sculptor and, of course, our 'own' George Wostenholm of Kenwood. He loved the Nether Edge area which in those days was entirely agricultural and quite some distance from Sheffield 'proper'. He was particularly fond of the two enormous oak trees just across the lane from the Brincliffe Oaks Public House (then a farm called Nether Edge — from which the district gets its name) and they were known as the Montgomery Oaks in his memory.

He died in 1854 at the great age of eighty-four and was honoured by a public funeral at the General Cemetery, the pall bearers being leaders of all the various religious denominations in the town. Recently his remains have been removed to the Cathedral graveyard.

Charles Peace

◆ Malcolm Weston

The name of Charles Peace is always linked to the Banner Cross area but, despite what many of us may have believed, he never actually lived in the area. Nor, contrary to local folklore, did he have any connection with the old Salt-Box Cottage and he certainly didn't carve the horse's head on the doorstep (if one ever actually existed).

Of one thing, however, there is no doubt. One evening in October 1878 Charles Peace shot and killed Arthur Dyson at his home at Banner Cross Terrace. (Banner Cross Terrace is still standing, the cottages having recently been converted into shops just below the Banner Cross Hotel. The Dyson's house, No 951, was the second above Marmion Road, now occupied by the Oriental Arts Centre.)

Peace was born in Angel Court, Nursery Street, on 14th May 1832. His father, formerly a collier of Burton-on-Trent, was a man of great strength, character and determination who worked with travelling fairs as a trainer of lions and tigers. Eventually settling in Sheffield he was variously a shoe repairer, coal dealer, carter and, finally, a publican in Water Lane. His mother, daughter of a naval surgeon, was many years younger than her husband.

The young Charles went to two schools — Pitsmoor School and Hebblethwaite's in Paradise Square. In both he was regarded as a poor scholar but good at anything which required ingenuity. At Sunday School he was known as a 'well behaved lad' but other reports refer to him as a strange hobgoblin of a child; a mixture of magpie and monkey who, nevertheless, became adept at all manner of pursuits and hobbies.

Originally apprenticed as a tin-smith he soon changed to the steel industry working as a roller at Millsands Rolling Mills. He was badly injured when a red hot steel strip went right through one of his legs and he had to endure an operation — without anaesthetic — for the removal of a shattered knee cap.

During a lengthy convalescence he was taught to play the violin by Joe Bethly, the watch maker of Division Street, and became a travelling musician and petty thief.

Over several years, Peace committed many burglaries notably one at Nether Edge where he stole seven pairs of boots and another at Brincliffe Edge which yielded a haul of jewellery. He served several terms of imprisonment and his

The last photograph taken of Charles Peace in 1879.

involvement in a mutiny at Chatham Prison earned him a flogging and deportation to a convict settlement in Gibraltar.

In 1864 he was released and returned to Sheffield where he set up a picture framing business in Kenyon Alley and later took a shop in West Street. (A picture framed by Peace is at Kelham Island Museum.)

In 1875 Peace and his wife (about whom little is known) went to live at 40 Victoria Place, Britannia Road, Darnall — next door to a Mr and Mrs Arthur Dyson who had recently returned from America, where Dyson had been a railway engineer. Peace was attracted to Mrs Dyson and set out to woo her with, it seems, some success and this was naturally the cause of much bad blood between the two men.

Eventually the Dysons moved to Banner Cross in the hope of escaping Peace's attentions and settled in Banner Cross Terrace.

Peace soon discovered that the Dysons had moved to Banner Cross and spent several nights in the area trying to locate the actual house. On the night of the murder, Peace accosted Mrs Dyson outside her house and, on hearing the commotion, her husband ran to her assistance.

Confronted with the burly figure of Arthur Dyson, Peace fired two shots from his pistol; the first hitting a wall and the second striking Dyson a fatal blow to the temple.

Local folklore maintains that Peace escaped up the little alley at the side of the Banner Cross Hotel but this is unlikely. An eye-witness, seventeen year old Thomas Wilson (one of *the* Wilsons?), heard the shots and saw a man run across the road from the house (Ecclesall Road) into the field on the opposite side (this would be in the area of the present Blair Athol Road).

The story of Peace's subsequent escapades would fill a book but, briefly, he hid in Ecclesall Woods for several days before setting out on a nationwide life of crime. He was finally captured in Blackheath (London) and brought back to Sheffield to stand trial for murder.

Passing through Darnall, he threw himself from the train at 50 mph but was so dazed from his injuries that he was easily recaptured.

Peace was defended by the Sheffield law firm of Clegg & Co and some years ago the writer was privileged to examine the original defence brief in their offices.

He was found guilty of the murder of Arthur Dyson on 4th February 1879 and hanged at Leeds a couple of weeks later.

Banner Cross, thirty years after Peace's time but still a rural scene.

John Cole of Prior Bank

◆ Joan Flett

In 1896 an anonymous writer wrote that John Cole 'now wears his eighty-two years with all the ease indicative of a sound constitution, visiting the warehouse daily and taking a keen interest in everything around him, and finding no enjoyment greater than that which he derives from the active supervision of his gardens at his charming residence, Prior Bank, where he has a considerable area under glass for the cultivation of rare and beautiful flowers'.

John was born in 1814 in Pickering, North Yorkshire, the eldest of three brothers. He served his apprenticeship in the drapery trade in Driffield. His master in Driffield had a brother in Sheffield and a year after he finished his apprenticeship John came to work for that brother in a shop in Angel Street. Three years later his employer was killed in a road accident and John went to work for Messrs T B and W Cockayne where he stayed until 1847 when he set up in business with his two brothers, Thomas and Skelton. As we know today the venture was extremely successful. On its site on the corner of Fargate and Church Street Cole Brothers shop expanded in 1869 and again in 1892. At the time of its jubilee in 1897 it was reported that 'the fine emporium is a type of those gigantic developments which so strikingly distinguish the drapery trade in modern times'. A sentiment which is equally apposite when applied to the modern building in Barkers Pool which was built in 1961.

Mr John Cole.

Cole Brothers' shop on its original site on the corner of Fargate and Church Street.

John bought Prior Bank from Benjamin Blonk Silcock in 1863 and shortly after bought additional land bordering Cherry Tree Road and Kingfield Road from Henry Newbould of Sharrow Bank. Some idea of the layout and extent of the house and gardens can be seen in sale plans of 1913. Like so many business men of the day John and his brothers were active in the life of the Town, particularly in the fields of religion and philanthropy. He was a prominent member of the Wesleyan Church and, until his death, worshipped at the Norfolk Street Chapel where he served in many capacities giving both time and money. He served on the Board of the Jessop Hospital for Women and, in 1861, was a founder member of the committee which set up The Association in Aid of the Deaf and Dumb. He was President of the Association for many years and, in 1885, together with other prominent businessmen, he bought land for the Association abutting Cross Burgess Street, Cambridge Street and Upper Charles Street.

John's wife died before him and he had no children. Although failing in health after 1896 he remained active and was at business only a month before he died on 15th May 1899. He was buried in the General Cemetery after a service in the Montgomery Chapel on Cemetery Road.

Prior Bank and its grounds in 1913.

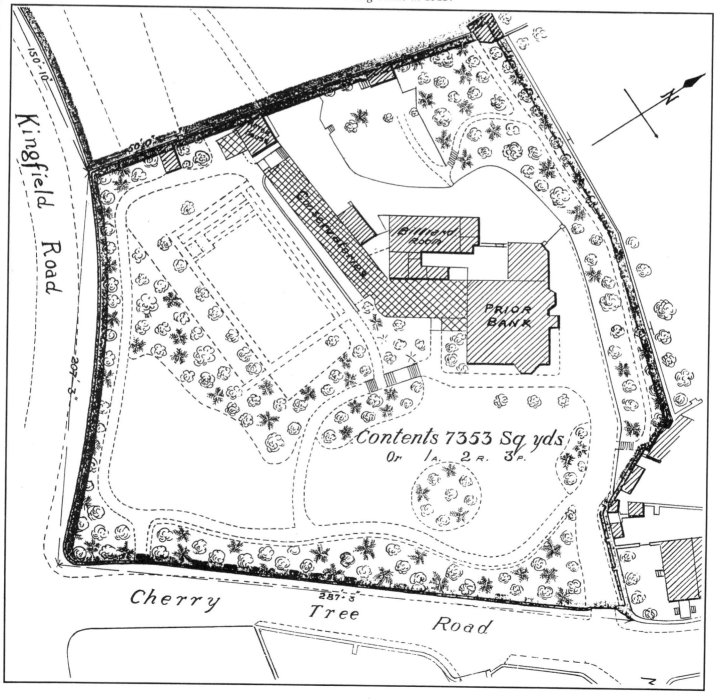

They built Nether Edge

The 'Self Builders' ◆ Giles Robinson

A great variety of people hired builders to design and erect houses for them in Sharrow and Nether Edge, and we can only select a few typical examples. All were men, which reflects the male dominance of suburban development and indeed of most areas of Victorian life.

HENRY ADAMS

Henry Adams was the head of the Refuge Assurance Company on Pinstone Street. He oversaw a great boom in the firm's business, and as a result he was able to build 119 Psalter Lane in 1874. Like most middle class Victorians he was a supporter of his local church. In his case it was the Primitive Methodists and he contributed towards the cost of many of their Sheffield buildings. He also financed a little speculative building, for example 33 and 35 Thornsett Road in 1902. Adams died in 1906 and his tomb can still be seen in the General Cemetery.

Henry Adams, a Victorian pillar of society.

T & J ROBERTS

Until recently T & J Roberts of Moorhead was one of Sheffield's best known department stores. In 1906 the Roberts described themselves as 'Drapers, silk mercers, dress and mantle makers, carpet warehousemen, cabinet makers and complete house furnishers'. They gave Sharrow two villas. The first was 1 Kenwood Bank, now a private school. It was intended for Thomas Roberts, one of the founders of the firm, but on his death it was built for his widow in 1899–1900. At the same time his son, Thomas Harland Roberts, was building 50 Kenwood Road. The two houses show the changing fashions in villa design, Thomas Harland Roberts having a very up-to-date house with the imitation half timbering which was to become so popular with suburbanites in the 1920s.

WILLIAM CRABTREE/JOHN BLYDE

The top two houses in Crescent Road seem to me to symbolise the ponderous Victorian villa. Lynthorpe, No 64, was built in 1867 for William Crabtree who ran a successful wallpaper hanging business. (The next occupant of No 64 was Robert Styring, mentioned in another article, who was for a time a business associate of William Crabtree). No 62 Crescent Road was built for John Blyde in 1865. Blyde was a scissor manufacturer, who built his own works near Wostenholm's Washington Works. In 1896 Blyde built himself another house with more extensive grounds at 84 Osborne Road, but did not enjoy his new propery long for he died in 1899.

EDWARD JAMES WOOLLEN

In 1883 Edward James Woollen founded the firm of Woollen and Co, signmakers, which is still in business. He moved into a new line of work when he established the Expert Advertising Company, and may have had other businesses under his control for he was said to be 'energetic to a degree which makes the average man uncomfortable'. Woollen seems truly to have been a man for the twentieth century. His personality certainly made him a perfect advertising man, as he considered that 'a frontal attack is the only way of carrying a position'. He was a pioneer of the early cinema in Sheffield and for a time owned his own picture house, The Tivoli, in Norfolk Street. He was an active member of the Sharrow Cycling Club, the Nether Edge Bowling Club and the Hallowes Golf Club near Dronfield. In 1912 Woollen had 41 Ashland Road built for him, and called it The Towers. He had previously lived at 44 Ashland Road and so would have been able to watch his new home being constructed from his windows.

JOSEPH PICKERING

Joseph Pickering founded the firm of Joseph Pickering, cardboard box manufacturers, which has just vacated its super factory near the bottom of the Moor. In 1902 he had 34 Kingfield Road built for himself in the Queen Ann style then fashionable. In 1903, the period when motor cars were first becoming popular, he added a garage. Another excellent example of an early garage, with a billiard room above it, was built in 1902 at 24 Wostenholm Road by Arthur Truelove, the chairman of Joseph Pickering.

GEORGE BUXTON

George Buxton was one of the many cutlery manufacturers who built up the thriving Sheffield cutlery industry in the nineteenth century. Between 1853 and 1856 he built himself Sharrow Villa, 27 Psalter Lane, which is a fine example of a house which aspires to the pretentions of its larger cousins such as Brinkcliffe Towers.

LOUIS HENRY OSBALDISTON

Louis Henry Osbaldiston was a file manufacturer, and the 1882 offices of his Challenge Works on Arundel Street are still standing. Osbaldiston was already resident in Nether Edge when he decided to build a new large house at the top of Ashland Road. This was Grange Court, No 71, with its ornamental stone gateway.

JOSEPH MITCHELL

Joseph Mitchell was a Sheffield architect who designed Heeley Church. In about 1855 he designed Meadow Bank (now Tintagel House, the Rudolph Steiner Centre) and intended to build himself a house on the Nether Edge estate. Instead he built 19 Kingfield Road in 1857 as his own residence, and presumably to his own design.

WILLIAM RYLAND

William Ryland, who ran Ryland's Electroplating Company, built Rye Lodge at 40 Ashland Road in about 1878. His house was filled with paintings, and when the collection was sold in 1887 it included works by Constable and Landseer.

HENRY CARR BOOTH

Henry Carr Booth was a table knife manufacturer. Spring Leigh, which was and still is one of the suburb's most impressive houses, was built for him in 1868 on the newly made Rundle Road. The grounds are said to have been laid out by Robert Marnock, the creator of the Botanic Gardens.

WILLIAM POOLE

One of Sheffield's numerous artists was William Poole, a portrait painter from Birmingham. His brother James also became an artist in Sheffield and was represented in Ryland's collection. In 1869 William Poole built 5 Oakdale Road.

EDWARD MAY

Edward May, of the firm William May and Co, Dyers and Cleaners, built 41 Rupert Road and Walter May of the same firm and family built 57 Nether Edge Road at about the same time in 1906. This company's dye works, built between 1892 and 1903 in Little London Road, is still standing.

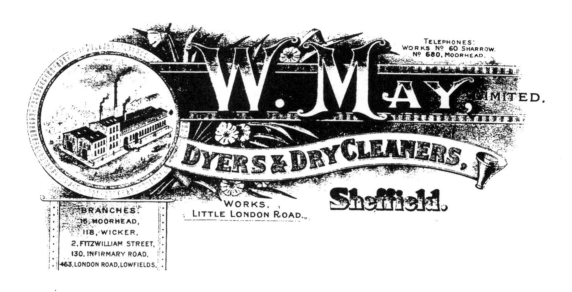

They built Nether Edge

The Local Speculative Builders ◆ Giles Robinson

A number of property developers in this area were not builders by trade.

JOHN LAW was curator of the Botanical Gardens until in 1858 he was forced to resign by the trustees who would no longer tolerate the amount of time he was devoting to speculative building and private commissions for landscape gardening. (Incidentally, Robert Marnock also left his post as the curator of the Botanical Gardens to pursue private landscape gardening work). Examples of houses built for Law in the 1850s are 3, 5 and 7 Williamson Road, and a very similar group at the top of Brocco Bank. These houses look as if they had been copied from the designs in one of the builders' manuals so popular in Victorian times, such as Samuel Hemmings' 'Designs for Villas, Parsonages and Other Houses' published in 1855.

WALTER JOHN CANDOW was an accountant, estate agent, rent collector and auctioneer. He lived for a time on Kenwood Road, and indulged in some speculative building on St Andrew's Road and Clifford Road from 1871 to 1877. He built the little cluster of villas (46–50 Clifford Road and 16–18 St Andrew's Road) which are squeezed as closely together as is possible while still remaining detached. With a partner he was also responsible for building, in 1876, the long terrace of three-storeyed houses, Nos 261–307 Abbeydale Road.

THOMAS MARRION was a brewer, who lived at Sharrow Grange on Sharrow Lane. In 1872 he laid out Grange Crescent, Grange Road and Grange Crescent Road (originally Marrion Road) and building began on these streets later in the same decade.

JOHN FIRTH, the steel manufacturer, owned the land which had originally been the estate of John Rodgers of Abbeydale House. He began to lay out the estate for building in 1867, starting with Bannerdale Road and Archer Road, but died shortly after. The work was continued by his trustees, who were members of the same family. Between 1896 and 1900 they laid out Rydal, Windermere, Thirlmere, Langdale, Buttermere, Crummock and Troutbeck Roads in the 'Lake District', and betwen 1899 and 1904 they continued with Swaledale, Coverdale and Fossdale Roads on the other side of Abbeydale Road.

JOHN WILKINSON ran a chemist and druggist business in Sheffield town centre. His family acquired the Priory Grange and its land from George Wostenholm in 1853. When Wilkinson took over the estate he developed it as terraced housing, demolishing the ancient Priory Grange in the process. He built the Old Priory Grounds, facing Priory Road, in 1877, and both Priory Avenue and Priory Cottages, which face Sharrow Lane, in 1878. Wilkinson himself lived at Priory Cottage, 219 Sharrow Lane, which was built in 1852 and is still standing though much altered. His building operations must have been profitable, as on his death he left £50,000 to charity.

'The Priory' where the Wilkinsons lived for many years. The central part of this complex building appears to be a very early structure, perhaps dating from the 15th century.

The site of 'The Priory' today. The old building was demolished in the development which took place in 1877, and this three-storied terrace was built in its place.

They built Nether Edge

◆ Giles Robinson

Although a handful of 'spec' builders were principally landowners or financiers, the majority were local builders. Many larger properties were built 'on spec' for the middle class but the main output was thousands of terraced houses. These ranged from small 'two up, two downs', like those on Fentonville Street, to the much larger and more imposing terraces on Sheldon Road. Though many of these lacked any great style or individuality they were nevertheless soundly built and have provided cosy, low-cost, low-maintenance housing for generation after generation. Unlike some recent award winning schemes they will continue to offer these benefits for many years to come.

JAMES SIVIL
James Sivil, the son of another builder, was born in 1863. He started life as a bricklayer, but worked his way up to become a builder and contractor and later a councillor and a Justice of the Peace. He started his own business with capital of less than £50 by building a pair of small cottages in Sharrow, and was able to take advantage of the terraced housing developments in Nether Edge, Sharrow, Heeley and Woodseats to make his fortune. In 1897 he built himself a villa at 31 Priory Road which is now used by a bridge club. Like Henry Adams, Sivil was a prominent supporter of the Primitive Methodist Church and its building programme in Sheffield. In his leisure time he enjoyed playing chess and like many local gentlemen he was a member of the Nether Edge Bowling Club. Examples of Sivil's work are houses in Langdale and Windermere Road built in 1896, 33–65 Sheldon Road (1899–1900) and 131–159 Sharrow Vale Road with 1–9 Westbrook Bank (1906). His family is still active in the Sheffield building trade.

James Sivil, builder and self-made man.

HENRY AND ROBERT BRUMBY

This father and son partnership built some of the area's more interesting houses; in particular the ones with the whimsical little corner towers at the top and bottom of Kenwood Park Road. A similar design stands at the corner of Crescent Road and Moncrieffe Road. Brumby started as a builder of terraced housing at Highfield — most of Kearsley Road was put up by him in the 1870s. For some time his son Robert lived in a Brumby built house at 10 Crescent Road.

Other Brumby built houses are 21–43 Kenbourne Road (1890–1893); 6–52 Montgomery Road (1882–1894); 1–3 Moncrieffe Road (1896); 49–51 Kenwood Park Road (1893); Nether Edge Market (1880) — this is the block of shops which includes the butchers, bakers and DIY shop. Brumby built all of Ladysmith Avenue (except The Edge) together with similar terraces in Barkers Road and Edgebrook Road between 1897–1900.

Brumby houses can be found at Ranmoor and also at Kenwood Avenue, the small back road off Montgomery Road where George Turton commissioned him to build the houses in 1892–4.

In 1889 Brumby built 11 houses and shops at the corner of Sharrow Lane and London Road (224–250 London Road).

House built by Henry and Robert Brumby, showing a typical corner turret.

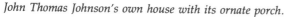

John Thomas Johnson's own house with its ornate porch.

JOHN THOMAS JOHNSON

John Thomas Johnson founded a joinery business with a works in Randall Street in the early 1870s, which produced doors, bay windows and other builders' items. In 1879 he built himself an imposing villa, Randall House, at 16 Moncrieffe Road which is now used at the Bye Group's offices. The ornate porch is probably a product of Johnson's works. In 1884 he built a terrace of houses, Nos 80–106 Club Garden Road, carrying stone plaques with names like Willow Mount, Holly Villa and Alder Place which commemorate the leafy hillside fast being submerged by bricks and mortar. In 1888 he built 15–53 Steade Road, a very solid looking terrace whose hallways are packed with examples of his firm's joinery. Later, from 1901–1903, Johnson built 34 Priory Road, 1–5 Agden Road, 9–19, 23 and 31 Thornsett Road and 34 Priory Road.

JOSEPH HUNT

Joseph Hunt was a local builder and contractor who built several houses on the Nether Edge estate. In 1872 he built 32 Oakhill Road and lived there for a time. Between 1880 and 1884 he built 2–18 Machon Bank road and 5, 42 and 44 Kingfield Road plus 121 Psalter Lane in 1874–76. The latter houses are all detached villas which show the simple variations of detail which a typical builder of the period would employ to give each house its individual character.

FRANCIS SMITH

Francis Smith built just a few houses in the area but, like most other small builders, probably sub-contracted for the larger concerns. In 1869 he built 7 Oakdale Road which was bought by John Richdale, the brewer. In 1870 he built 22 Brincliffe Edge Road and the following year finished 6 and 8 Herbert Road. Like most Victorian suburban houses these are designed to be viewed only from the front, which explains the paradox of the neat, prim fascias but tatty and messy rear elevations. Like most small builders without their own manufacturing facilities, Smith used standard ready-made doors and windows and so on.

7 Oakdale Road, built in 1869 by Francis Smith and sold to John Richdale the brewer. T & J Roberts' removal van stands outside, and this picture was probably taken after Richdale's death in 1903. The house behind was built by William Poole whose family lived there until the 1920s, and further away is the Brincliffe Oaks Hotel.

The Nether Edge Bowling Club

in Victorian Times   ◆ Janet Hartley

A gentle perusal of the leather-bound, elegantly hand-written, early minute books of the Nether Edge Bowling Club plunge the reader eerily into the often surprising detail of local Victorian social life and manners.

In the middle of 1867 a group of wealthy businessmen leased an area of land adjacent to Nether Edge Road for sixty years and erected a fine, one-storey stone building with an immense south-facing bay window overlooking the new green. A keeper had been installed, one hundred and fifty shares of five pounds each were being sold to all who wished to be members and a Committee of Management was put in charge of the organisation of events.

Each year the bowling season began with the Opening Match. In 1875 this was arranged for the 26th May 'play to commence at three o'clock and a dinner to be provided by the Greenkeeper at 3/- each member, to be on the table by seven o'clock.

After the addition of a second storey to the clubhouse in 1874 to accommodate two billiard tables, this game became equally popular and by the end of the century matches were being arranged with other Sheffield gentlemen's clubs of the day such as the Atheneum, the Reform Club and the Ecclesall Conservative Club. In September 1896 a notice went out that 'on the 25th instant an Exhibition Match at billiards will be played between the celebrated cueist E Diggle and Mr W G Whittaker, a member of this club'. If you climb the narrow staircase, guided by its heavy, rounded wooden banister and enter the long room with its original fireplaces and hugely impressive black, leather-upholstered benches stretching along each wall, you might expect these two gentlemen to appear at any moment and begin their game, so vivid is the heavy Victorian atmosphere of the place. To this day women are not allowed across the threshold.

Card games played in the saloon below (for very small stakes only) included flop, napoleon, loo and whist. Chess and backgammon both had their vogue.

Amongst the professions of the Victorian members were those of organ-builder, journalist, music teacher, pawnbroker, steel manufacturer, chemist and accountant. The saloon in which these gentlemen enjoyed each other's company must have been heavy with the fumes of smoke and liquor. Beer, porter and cigars, casks of brandy (£28 19s. 0d. a time), whisky and gin, gallons of port wine and bottles of Médoc (at four shillings per dozen) were kept in constant supply. Here weary businessmen and professionals relaxed in an idyllic green retreat in their new suburb away from the dingy factories and cramped offices over which they presided in the city centre. The club must also have been a welcome escape from Victorian domestic life with its large, troublesome families, servants and strict social etiquette.

Women and children were, however, allowed into the generally hallowed saloon more often than one might have imagined. There was an Annual Ball (or 'Late Assembly', as it became known) for which tickets cost 1s. 6d. each for members, and for guests 2s. (ladies) and 2s. 6d. (gentlemen). A piano was hired in the winter for four months, holland was purchased 'for covering the Saloon floor for dancing', and concerts were arranged. In 1898 the President of the day, Mr Palmer, 'offered to give a garden party, each member to be allowed to introduce one lady'. We are not given any details of this event but it must have been an extremely lavish affair as, in order to thank Mr Palmer for his generosity, the Committee presented him with his portrait for providing 'the Red Letter day in the annals of the club'. Other family events were 'a Legerdemain (magic) Entertainment to be given by Mr Maurice Chenfeldt, admission 6d.' and an 'Incognito Minstrels Concert'. For the younger members of the family there was an annual Christmas party and Juvenile Ball and other excitements such as magic lantern shows and something described as 'dissolving views for the amusement of the children'.

'Soirée dansante' will evoke in your mind's eye a refined Victorian evening where the gentlemen have exquisite manners in the presence of their elegantly-gowned and coiffed ladies. The minutes of January 1875 tell us, however, that when Mrs Holiday protested she had bought her ticket earlier in the evening, a certain member told her, 'he doubted it, that is would not do for him and rudely laid his hand upon her shoulder'. End-of-evening punch-ups seemed a regular happening after these events. In November 1877 the secretary

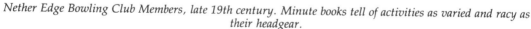

Nether Edge Bowling Club Members, late 19th century. Minute books tell of activities as varied and racy as their headgear.

was obliged to write to a member complaining he had been seen taking part in 'riotous, disorderly and unseemly proceedings in the refreshment room here at the close of the soirée dansante'.

The frequent letters to the Committee about fellow members' behaviour give us a lively picture of a typical evening in the saloon. A Mr Wigfull describes how he was 'most grossly insulted by Mr John Jee in the presence of several members'. He was in the saloon when Mr Jee came up to him, drunk, and said he would pull his coat collar off and called him 'a liar and a scamp'. Arthur Wainwright's name appears regularly in letters complaining about his drunken and disorderly behaviour. He finally gave up apologising to the committee and decided to have the last word by sending in his resignation, adding 'if you or them' (the members who had complained about him) 'know anyone wishful to purchase a share for which I gave your committee £5, then they may have one cheap from, Yours faithfully, Arthur Wainwright'. It was recorded in the minutes that 'the committee are pleased to hear that Mr Wainwright is no longer to continue as a member', and they heaved a sigh of relief, no doubt hardly believing their eyes when he re-appeared on the green! After he had paid a fine of five shillings he was not heard of again.

At the meeting of March 1896 a letter from Mr Tate was read out alleging that when he asked Mr Fairburn to be quiet in the billiard room during a tournament the latter became abusive 'garnishing his remarks with such choice epithets as "d-----d swine" and "billiard sharp".' When Tate called him a blackguard, the other man grabbed hold of his coat and tried to hit him! The committee demanded a written apology from the aggressive Mr Fairburn who duly sent a terse note. This effort did not satisfy the secretary who replied by drafting him a specimen apology covering all the necessary points. Fairburn, obviously a man of spirit, wrote, 'I can candidly assure you that I am not going to sign the abject apology that you think fit to put upon me for the sake of a man like Mr Tate. If you want me to make the club a present of my share, take it. I shan't trouble the place and it is not my intention to mix with the lot who compose it again.' It is a tribute to the long-serving secretary, Mr Edmund Garlick, that he was eventually able to make peace between the two sides of the dispute.

The greenkeeper (or steward, as he later became known) of the club had a very large number of duties in these early days. As well as mowing the green and occasionally spreading 'a quantity of Beatson's Manure and Charcoal Dust', he served the drinks and generally waited on at the call of numerous bells installed throughout the premises.

Presumably aided by his wife, he also did the cleaning and prepared the various teas and dinners required by the members. During its first years the club seems to have had some unlucky experiences. At a meeting in November 1875 it was agreed 'that the seven bottles of brandy produced before the committee be confiscated, it having been diluted with water by the greenkeeper'. In June 1882, referring to Samuel Wilkinson who followed, 'the secretary stated that he had collected nine subscriptions and absconded with the money'. A real fiend this — he left his wife behind to face the music! On the 17th June 1882 a Mr Atkin was appointed after the understandable precaution of paying Mr Deans five shillings 'for expenses on his enquiring as to the character of the new steward'. By 1895 complaints were being received about a new incumbent, a Mr Roberts, referring to 'the proper cleaning and disinfecting of the urinals, the due supervision of the fires, the delay in giving change, the refilling and keeping supplied the matchstands', making one wonder how long he was going to last!

In spite of all the difficulties, the committee worked steadfastly on, determined to keep the club well-decorated and up-to-date. In February 1894 they agreed to have 'the use of the Telephone wire and Instrument at the rent of £10 per annum' from the National Telephone Company Ltd.

The fact that it is the only outside event to be mentioned in these early minute books gives some idea of the emotion aroused throughout the country by the assassination of the Duke of Devonshire's son in 1882. Lord Frederick Cavendish had accepted the post of Irish Secretary under Gladstone. A few hours after arriving in Dublin to take up his duties, he and Mr Burke, the under-secretary, were stabbed to death by four men in Phoenix Park. At the annual meeting of the Club it was unanimously agreed that the following letter should be sent:

'The members desire to express their deep sympathy with Lady Cavendish, his Grace the Duke of Devonshire and the other members of his family and also with the relatives of the late Mr Burke in the great loss they sustained by the horrible and treacherous crime committed in Dublin on Saturday 6th May 1882.'

Otherwise, for the members of this exclusive club, a peaceful haven set high above Nether Edge Road, the century drew quietly to a close as the invitations went out at the end of the season:

'Sir, I beg to inform you that the closing match at bowls will be played on Thursday afternoon at 4 o'clock. A dinner will be provided at 6 o'clock at 1/6 each, to be followed by a Smoking Concert, your presence being cordially invited.'

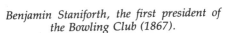

Benjamin Staniforth, the first president of the Bowling Club (1867).

Old houses at the top of Glen Road

◆ Janet Hartley

A sale plan dated 1866 for land in Glen Road announced that 'these plots are in the midst of unequalled scenery, the land is rich in quality and the approach from the town is pleasant — through the well-roaded estates belonging to George Wostenholm, Esq'. By the end of the century a few small but substantial villas had begun to form the character of this north-east corner of the Montgomery Land Society. On the 1892 map (charmingly tinted in pink and blue) Glen Road ends abruptly as a cul-de-sac just after the junction with Rupert Road and from there the view was open fields down to Abbeydale Road. The Edge Brook is shown rising to the surface about half way down Glen Road, flowing through the bottom of the back gardens on the north side, down through the fields, under a small bridge and on past the side of the Broadfield Hotel (then standing isolated at the edge of fields, surrounded by a large garden and trees), where it disappeared under the road before reappearing finally to join the Sheaf. I searched for traces of the brook which must have been a very attractive feature of the area but, sadly, it has been completely culverted below the surface.

The Edge Brook once flowed by the Broadfield Hotel, Abbeydale Road. Its original Victorian glass and woodwork are still worth a visit.

Although almost every aspect of the 'unequalled scenery' has now disappeared, from the detailed old maps I could see that the Victorian houses at the junction of Glen Road and Nether Edge Road have remained almost unchanged in their immediate surroundings — garden layout, outbuildings — for over a hundred years. In fact they seem still to retain that atmosphere which their Victorian owners aspired to create — solid respectability in a pleasant, green retreat. I was curious to know who those families were who had first been drawn there, where they had come from and what work they did.

No 7 Glen Road, known then as 'Edge View', is a small, double fronted, stone built villa with a fine wooden staircase and solid internal shutters. It was originally owned in the 1870s by John Biggin, a silversmith who had a workshop in Milk Street where he employed thirteen men and four boys, a reasonably large establishment for those days. His wife, Louisa, appears to have been one of those robust Victorian women who could easily rival any of the present day feminists. At his death she took over the business and was still running it in her late fifties while Mary Vickers, from Nether Green, lived in as her general servant and looked after the house. By the end of the 1880s, George Tandy, comb manufacturer, had bought Edge View. His father had lived in Burgess Street in the 1860s but the family business in Highfield (which from the advertisement in Kelly's Directory sounds quite a grand

establishment, with its London warehouse) had allowed the son to graduate to the outer suburbs where life was much more pleasant than in the dark, narrow streets of the city centre with their cramped, back-to-back houses and open sewers. In a few years Tandy was gone to perhaps even more lush pastures and the house was inhabited until the end of the century by a succession of shadowy widows.

No. 7 Glen Road. Its past recalls a long-forgotten Sheffield trade.

The neighbouring house up the hill has caused much speculation by its individuality. Whereas all the other houses of its period in the area are built of the locally quarried sandstone, No 5, 'Glenlea' and its front wall have pretensions. They are built of a stange, whitish stone which the present owner explained to me is Aberdeen granite and the same material of which Kenwood is constructed. There are rumours that this small family house was built of the 'left-overs' from George Wostenholm's great house. Even the distinctive Gothic Revival style of No 5, with its impressive stone window frames attractively ornamented and its large corner blocks is very reminiscent of the mansion built thirty years before. I have to admit I was unable to establish any facts behind this intriguing similarity.

The first owner at the beginning of the 1880s was Benjamin Beeley, the former proprietor of the Washington Arms on Washington Road where the Montgomery Land Society held its early meetings. He was clearly a successful victualler because by the age of forty-nine he had retired and bought this charming house where he lived with his wife Elizabeth and their servant, Jane (aged 13). By 1890 the owner was Samuel Staniforth, a 'manufacturer of table, butchers', sword, spear, hunting, dagger and cook knife blades', and some of his original work premises still stand in Carver Street, though at this time he had other forges at Backfields and Stannington. You feel that Staniforth was very proud of his 'little Kenwood', its richly moulded ceilings, solid doors and lovely staircase. He must have delighted in the craftsmanship of the globe garden lamp and wrought iron gates with their unusual gothic motif harmonising so beautifully with the house. He must have loved, too, the glowing colours and intricate design of the glasswork as he came through his front door every evening after days spent in the murky blade forges.He had his name carved in stone in front of the house and his own splendid billiard room, complete with fireplace, built in the grounds in 1896. The outside of this building is finished off with the grand Victorian flourish of an intricate roof-top finial which stands out faultless today against the open sky. Samuel Staniforth's spirit lingers here in Glen Road and his name lives on at the works in Alma Street where the company moved in 1982. The personnel at the new premises are very proud to tell you that their exclusive range of cooks' and butchers' knives, carrying the original Staniforth Smithfield Bull trademark, is admired and sold all over the world. It is pleasing to know that his professional reputation is being perpetuated under his own name and that the home he loved is cherished and preserved.

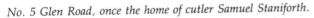

No. 5 Glen Road, once the home of cutler Samuel Staniforth.

Samuel Staniforth's abandoned forge building on Carver Street.

Across the road on the corner is No 11 Nether Edge Road, a much plainer, sandstone house with its own individual charm. The double-fronted façade, with a large arch over the front door and a bay window to the right, always seems to look with a friendly expression out on to the main road. In November 1869 William Howe of Barker Nook applied to the council for permission to construct outbuildings, stables and coach-house and these remain intact at the top of the wide yard to the rear. It is not difficult to imagine Mr Howe (retired table knife manufacturer living on his income), his wife Caroline and two daughters Dora and Margaret proudly riding out from their brand new house in a smart carriage and clattering along Montgomery Road into town. The house has retained its large, walled and well-kept garden to the right and one imagines that the neat little orchard there today is not much different from in Howe's time. Nothing seems to have been altered and the north-facing gable end which was apparently being affected by subsidence was skilfully dismantled and rebuilt during 1987. I could find little detail about the Howe family other than they must have liked the house and the district as they stayed there for nearly fifty years, Miss Margaret Howe still being in residence in 1913.

The house on the opposite corner, No 9 Nether Edge Road, was built slightly later and has rather a stolid air about it. Its stonework is plain (no fancy, gothic revival nonsense here!) and the only light touch is on the pretty porch door which was probably a later addition. On all the old maps of the area, however, Guzerat House is always boldly shown and this strange name holds the key to the very different story this house has to tell. The history of the other houses gives a picture of Victorian Sheffield, its trades and local people; No 9 Nether Edge Road reflects the Victorian era in a much wider sense.

Thomas Nash was born in 1837 in Swindon, Wiltshire. It was there in 1843 that Brunel opened the first important engine depot and repair shop of the Great Western Railway which ran between London and Bristol. That was how the history of this great railway town began and in the ensuing years many classic locomotives of the great Victorian railway era were to be built there. It is not surprising that Thomas Nash was taken up as a young man with the excitement of these new ventures and he became a railway engineer. By his mid-twenties he had married a local woman from Corsham and they had travelled together to Surat on the West coast of India, just north of Bombay, on the railway line to Delhi. At that time the imperial British Government and private companies were beginning to

No. 9 Nether Edge Road — Guzerat House. Research uncovered the story behind this exotic name.

build railway lines and together, by 1880, had built over 8,000 miles of track. Thus Thomas Nash became part of the British 'raj' which saw its role in India as a provider of communications and irrigation so that private agricultural, industrial and commercial enterprise could flourish. Nash's first child, Annie Sophia, was born in Surat. By his early thirties the engineer was back in his home town of Swindon for a while but he was soon on his pioneering travels again and by 1872 was settled in Glasgow. At this period there were five great railway companies based in Scotland, the North British and the Caledonian being the largest and this was the decade when Midland passenger trains first ran to Glasgow and Edinburgh, the Tay Bridge was opened and the Glasgow Central Station was built. Thomas Nash eventually decided to settle in Sheffield, probably because of its central position in the country, its growing steel industry and the fact that the Yorkshire Engine Company and others had important locomotive works in the city. By 1880 he had an office in Fitzalan Square and his profession is recorded as 'consulting civil engineer'.

He named his home in Nether Edge 'Guzerat House' after the area where he had lived in India. By then his family consisted of his wife, Mary, daughters Annie Sophia and Jane Elizabeth and son William Thomas. With the wide engineering experience he had gained over the previous twenty years he founded the company which some years later moved to premises in Blonk Street and became known as The Sheffield Testing Works. This company was concerned with devising new testing methods for all types of metals, an essential service if Sheffield was to maintain its high standards of steelmaking. In separate offices in Blonk Street he owned another company, Thomas Nash and Son, Inspecting Engineers. At the end of the century British capital and industry provided the railway engines, coaches and wagons for South America and it was Thomas Nash's engineers who did the inspection work of the rolling stock before it was sent abroad. He employed forty or fifty inspectors at offices in Manchester, Glasgow, Middlesbrough, Workington, Bristol and London — all great Victorian railway cities. Buenos Aires Great Southern, Buenos Aires Western, Central Argentines, Autofagasta and Bolivia Railways were some of the companies for which Britain provided rolling stock. When, at the beginning of the 1900s, the Latin American companies found that the railways were benefiting the European investors more than themselves by providing markets for European goods and draining money from their governments, their countries began to nationalize them. There was a great reduction in demand at the Sheffield steelworks which had provided thousands of wheels, tyres and axles. The great railway companies like Beyer Peacock at Manchester and George Stephenson at Newcastle were badly hit by this event. Thomas Nash was forced to close all his offices outside Sheffield and concentrate on the Testing Works.

Inspection work on winding gear in the collieries was developed. The company's reputation grew and it obtained work on metal testing from all over the country.

When I contacted the Sheffield Testing Works I was told to visit Mr Leonard Evans, now ninety-six, a former technical director who had worked there for seventy years, starting as an engineering apprentice in 1906. When he joined the company, Mr Evans told me, Thomas Nash junior had taken over from his father and I was shown a photograph of the splendid six cylinder Napier his employer owned at the time, the cause of many a speeding fine. "The chassis had been brought from London by train and taken to the Craven Carriage and Wagon Company at Darnall to have the body fitted. It was one of the finest cars in Sheffield." The younger Thomas Nash also lived in Nether Edge, at 182 Psalter Lane, now Constance Grant's Dancing School.

I am indebted to Mr Evans for foregoing details of the Nash inspecting company. He also gave me a vivid description of the life of a young man at the Blonk Street Works at the beginning of the century. "We worked from 6 am to 5 pm for five shillings (25p) a week and often did four hours overtime without pay, making up a 53 hour week." On his way to work from his home in Attercliffe, he would call in at 'The Wilberforce', a coffee house on the Wicker, for a penny cup of coffee. An additional tot of rum cost thruppence. "We were allowed half an hour for breakfast at 8 am and an hour for lunch at midday. The foreman used to give us sixpence (2½p) to get ourselves some tea before overtime. On Saturday we worked from 6 am to 1 pm." Just down the street from the Testing Works, however, was the famous Alexandra Theatre overhanging the River Don. "At nine o'clock, after overtime, we'd go along to see the second house. There were orange sellers outside with oranges in big baskets — three a penny. I remember a melodrama called, I think, 'The Silver King' and the villain was 'hanged' on stage. It was fourpence a seat." By the age of twenty-one the young men had completed their very strict apprenticeship and would be earning 30 shillings (£1.50) a week, with no holiday pay. Women, except a cleaner, were not employed at the Testing Works until after the Second World War. In 1962 Mr Evans helped the company to move to its present works and offices in Nursery Street.

Thomas Nash, who had entered so fully into the spirit of the Victorian age, lives on in the continuing scientific work of the enterprise he founded. His company is still very much part of the engineering life of the city and the country.

The discoveries I had made about these four houses were an inspiration. This area and its buildings are worthy of preservation because of their own charm and character but also because they were the loved houses of people who, by their hard work and vision, have a direct influence on our lives today.

The charming No. 11 Nether Edge Road, unchanged since the days of first owner William Howe.

The Brinkcliffe Tower Estate

◆ Audrey Stanton

There is evidence of a farm on this site, owned by a William Staniforth, Church Burgess, as long ago as 1587 and over the centuries it passed through many hands, including those of Abraham Ibbotson of Arundel in Sussex, Samuel Staniforth of Mosborough and George Woodhead of Highfields.

In 1852, James Wilson, solicitor and Clerk to the Cutlers' Company, late of Highfield House and Broomhall Street became the new owner and started to build a fine new home, leaving the old farmhouse (at the junction of Brinkcliffe Edge Road and Quarry Lane) as a lodge keeper's cottage.

A Newspaper report in November 1925 gives the following description:

'Brinkcliffe Tower was built by James Wilson, a descendant of the Wilsons of Broomhead Hall. It stands some 500 feet above sea level and is beautifully situated and laid out. Architecturally, the house is a combination of Early English and Renaissance styles and has the reputation of being the most strongly built house in Sheffield. The walls are of very great thickness and the basements are excavated in solid rock. One of its features is a lofty tower, from which wide views of the whole district are to be obtained.' (The mounds set with trees were supposedly constructed later, to hide the view of the Workhouse at Nether Edge!) 'The grounds and park were from the first very tastefully laid out and planted with a great variety of trees. These are now well established and make the long, winding drive from Brinkcliffe Edge Road a very pleasant approach to the house.'

After James Wilson's death in 1867, the estate was owned by George Marples, a carver and gilder, of Fargate and Church Street. He was agent to the London Art Union and kept an establishment known as 'The Artists' Repository'.

In 1902 the house and its twelve acres of parkland were purchased by Alderman Robert Styring, LLD, JP, one of Sheffield's most prominent citizens, and a leading member of Cemetery Road Congregational Church — now demolished and the site of SKF Dormer Tools. He had married Annie Frances Hovey, whose father owned a drapers and outfitters shop in Angel Street, and they began their married life in 1880 in a house on Crescent Road. With their two sons and two daughters they loved walking over the moors and spent as much time as possible at their country retreats — the first was Knoutchley Farm between Froggatt and Eyam, and later they rented Moorseats near Hathersage. It was not unusual for Robert to leave his office in the centre of town at the end of a busy day and walk all the way to join his wife and family for a weekend in Derbyshire; but these days came to an end with the acquisition of Brinkcliffe Tower, which was to provide the perfect setting for their busy social life. The grounds often echoed to the sound of laughter as they entertained their friends and various religious and philanthropic associations. When he was Lord Mayor, in 1907, more than 600 guests attended a Garden Party and what a wonderful occasion it must have been with many of the gentlemen in frock coats and tall, grey top-hats, and the ladies displaying all the latest fashions. (The Sheffield Daily Independent gave a vivid report of the proceedings which is unfortunately far too detailed to be published here.)

Mrs Styring died in March 1925 and at a special meeting of the City Council in the following November, her husband handed over the title deeds of the Brinkcliffe Edge Estate to the

Brinkcliffe Tower in the Styrings' time.

citizens of Sheffield as a lasting memorial to his dear wife. His original intention was to remain in residence himself until his death, but in the autumn of 1935 he decided to retire to Paignton in Devon and most of the grounds were then opened to the public, but the house stood empty for a number of years. It was eventually used briefly as a dormitory for a girls' school before being requisitioned by the Army during the Second World War.

In 1960 it opened as a residential home for the elderly, having been adapted and extended by the J G Graves Charitable Trust. The grounds, now popularly called Chelsea Park, continue to be a source of great pleasure to the local population, almost completely untouched by the passage of time. Long may this continue.

A wintry day in Brinkcliffe Tower grounds, now Chelsea Park. The mound which hid the workhouse from view can be seen behind the sheep.

The great garden party held at Brinkcliffe Tower in 1907, when Robert Styring was Lord Mayor.

Edwardian high summer: a page from the Styring family album.

My first school

◆ Ruby McDonald

I am going a long way back down Memory Lane in recounting my first school days.

As far as I can recall there were three 'dame schools' in Sharrow then. Miss Cawood's was on Crescent Road, Miss Wood's was on Psalter Lane and the one I attended was on Sheldon Road. This last was called Sharrow High School and to my way of thinking it was the best known of the three.

The school occupied part of a large semi-detached house which stood next to the Stores where new flats have recently been built. The rest of the house was the home of Miss Jackson, who ran the school with her sister Mrs Foxon, her niece Miss Foxon and several teachers who came in daily. Pupils started at five. Boys usually left at ten or eleven, many going on to King Edward's School, but the girls stayed on into their teens.

The curriculum included the usual subjects, with great emphasis on the three Rs. Painting and music were extras and special fees were paid for them.

The day started with prayers at 9.00 am, followed by lessons until the break at 11.00 am for milk, another extra. We went home for lunch at 12.30 pm (no such thing as a school meal in those days), then back to school from 2.00 to 4.00 pm. Half term consisted of only one day's holiday on the Monday, not a whole week, but pupils were allowed a half day's holiday for their birthday if this fell in term time. This concession was very much appreciated!

We had very primitive gymnastic exercises; no apparatus, just 'ups and downs'. Out of doors we played an equally primitive form of volley ball.

We took the Junior Oxford examinations and the Royal Drawing Society exams. When music pupils were thought to have reached the required standard for an exam they were taken down to Wilson Peck's studios at Barkers Pool to be vetted by the famous Miss Marie and Miss Elsie Foxon who were eminent local music teachers. This ordeal, I might add, was far worse than taking the actual exam. The Misses Foxon were both large and imposing ladies with enormous bouffant hair styles who dressed in long and flowing gowns reminiscent of a bygone age, and they appeared very alarming to young pupils who were already shaking at the knees with nervousness.

The most exciting occurence I remember was the celebration of the end of the First World War. The Nether Edge Hall was taken for our breaking-up party in December 1918, and all the pupils took part in some form of entertainment. I remember that, although I was very much a beginner, I had to play 'The Bluebells of Scotland' extremely shakily, not being helped by having my mother and my much older brother in the audience.

In conclusion I must add that the grounding given by this school was excellent, and was of great help to me when I went on to boarding school at the age of fourteen.

Looking down Sheldon Road past the shops of Nether Edge Market and the tram terminus, Sharrow High School can be seen in the background.

The shops of Nether Edge

◆ remembered by Mrs M Jackson and Mrs E Jarman

The shops in Nether Edge and Sharrow were rather more numerous in the 1920s and 1930s than they are today. As well as the shops at the tram terminus, which we know today as the Nether Edge traffic lights, there was a cluster of small shops near the Union Hotel.

Opposite Mrs Jarman's family home on the corner of Union Road and Osborne Road there was a grocer's shop, just as there is today. It was run by Mr Bensley, who lived on Chelsea Road and came to the shop each day on his bicycle. Round the corner from the Union Hotel, in Machon Bank Road, was a little shop made out of the front room of a house and kept by a dignified old lady called Miss Kitchin. She sold sweets and it was there that Mrs Jarman spent her Saturday pennies as a child.

Further down the hill, on the corner of Barker's Road, was a greengrocer's kept by Mr and Mrs Boult. At the top corner of Violet Bank Road and Machon Bank Road was a plumber's called Cullabine's, and on the opposite corner was a grocer's so crammed full of cardboard boxes and cartons of goods that there was scarcely room for the customers.

A little further on the big Machon Bank garage was originally the tram shed. The trams ran until midnight, and started again early in the morning. The return fare was 2½d. (one new penny), Mrs Jackson remembers, and the tickets were pink and white striped.

The pastrycook's, now Turner's bakery shop, belonged at one time to Mrs Calvin. Her cakes were delicious and she also bought beef steak from Tym's the butcher's and turned it into potted meat which she put into little glass dishes, covered with melted butter and sold at 4½d. a quarter. Later Clifford Cowling kept this shop.

Henry Tym ran the butcher's shop which still bears his name, and his brother William was the local milkman who travelled in a horse drawn trap and poured the milk straight from a measuring can into your kitchen jug.

The corner shop in Nether Edge Market, which is a DIY store today, was then Knowles the grocer's. This was a superior establishment, with chairs where the ladies sat while giving their orders for delivery. There were big tins of biscuits from which you chose what you wanted, and sugar was weighed out of sacks into heavy blue paper bags which were then neatly folded over. Everything was sold loose . . . flour, lentils, dried peas and so on. They also sold poultry and game. Mrs Jackson's mother usually got her rabbits free as her father was allowed to shoot them on the farm where he worked, but once she went into Knowles to buy a rabbit for one shilling. The shopkeeper took it away and skinned it on a wooden slab at the back of the shop. When he brought it back her mother asked him what he was going to do with the skin and he said 'Keep it!' Now that skin was worth 4d., so she told him he could keep the skin and the rabbit too, and walked out of the shop. She would have cleaned the skin with salt and pegged it out on a board to dry; then it would have been used in making a rug.

Next door was originally a greengrocer's, run by the Walkers who lived in Osborne Road. Later this shop was taken over by Mrs Amies, who lived in a flat over the sweet shop on the opposite corner. For many years she sold clothes, haberdashery and wool at Nether Edge, but she had another more glamorous profession as a singer, under the name of Bessie Unwin. Her brother Booth Unwin, who lived in Montgomery Road, also sang at concerts and Masonic dinners. This shop still sells wool and haberdashery today.

The old chemist's shop on Nether Edge Road, with Hay's wine merchants beyond.
Is that a pump on the left outside the entrance to the Bowling Club?

Tram Terminus Netheredge

Mr Cammack ran the gentlemen's hairdressers next door to the Bowling Club. Hedley Cammack, his son, continued working there until his retirement in September 1987 after sixty one years at the shop! At one time there was a ladies' salon at the back run by old Mr Cammack's daughter-in-law.

Across the road from the Byron Hotel was another grocer's shop, also full of tins of biscuits and sacks of other produce. In the stockroom at the back Mr Ibbotson, president of the Funeral and Sick Benefit Society, sat on Monday nights to collect subscriptions. Mrs Jackson remembers her father calling her in from playing on Needham's Fields below Brincliffe Edge, to go down and pay his weekly dues of 6d.

Across the top of Glen Road was the Nether Edge Hall, with tennis courts and a pavilion at the back of it. Here a barrage balloon was flown during the Second World War, and the WAAFs who ran the unit were billeted in the Hall.

Where the travel agency now stands was for many years a chemist's, Smith and Hill's, which had big glass bottles filled with brightly coloured liquids in the window. One of the two men who kept it was small and pale, but the other seemed to Mrs Jackson as a child to be a great bearded giant of a man. Later this was still a chemist's shop, but under the name of Cook and Dale. There has always been an off-licence where Threshers now stands, but the present laundrette used to be a shoe shop run by Mr Greaves and the Health Food Stores was

an ironmonger's kept by Mr Holgate and his sister.

Until a few years ago the Post Office had always been where the greengrocer's is today, and next door was a ladies' and children's outfitters kept by the two Misses Hubbard, who dressed in black bombazine in the traditional fashion of their time. The dentist's surgery is a very recent newcomer. In Mrs Jackson's childhood she was taken to the doctor's on Lyndhurst Road when she had a toothache. The white haired doctor wore a stained frock coat and his surgery was not at all clinical, as there were spades, forks and other garden tools stored in it!

There has always been a sweet and tobacco shop on the corner of Nether Edge and Sheldon Roads and next door a branch of Gowers the grocers stood where the Abbey Glen cleaners is now. There were no shops further down Sheldon Road, until later two of the larger houses were converted into a fishmonger's and a delicatessen, and the Co-operative Stores opened a butcher's shop with a grocery department next door. Across Sheldon Road in a stone lean-to with a slate roof there lived, or at least slept, a charming man called Mr Coffey who sold newspapers. His sister also sold papers from a wooden box on wheels.

As Mrs Jarman says, the shops in 'Nether Edge Market' and around it have had to change over the years to suit the times, but their owners can still provide you with all the necessities of life and, above all, with the traditional, personal and friendly service of a village store.

The way it was . . .

Among the regulars at the newly re-furbished Byron Hotel (which was originally a private house) is Keith Mellor of Machon Bank. He can remember the good old days when a certain lady customer at Orme's the grocers (now the DIY shop on the corner) used to ask for one kipper to be delivered and when, at the Heeley Baths, you could relax in a cubicle after a steam bath and summon a waiter to bring you tea-cakes and coffee. He can remember, too, when the Byron used to be an off-sales shop selling only jugged beer from the present tap room. Finally a proper pub, at first it sold beer only and had a six-day licence. To get a wines and spirits and a seven-day licence two ladies had to give their signatures and in this case they were Mr Mellor's mother and her friend (who lived at No. 11 Nether Edge Road).

A Telephonist's Job in the Twenties   Mrs M Jackson

When I was at school at Abbeydale, I took an examination at Fitzalan Square to become a telephonist. I had a medical examination on Sharrow Lane at Highfield House opposite the Community Centre as it is now, where the Sitwells once lived. Then I went to Broad Street for an interview and had to take dictation by telephone, also handwriting and sums etc. Then I waited for the result. A representative came to visit my mother to see what sort of a home I came from! I was then accepted as a girl probationer at 13s. 6d. a week. I was on probation for two years. I had to pass other examinations before I became a fully-fledged Post Office Telephonist and then earned 16s. 9d. per week.

We were not allowed to wear any jewellery nor to have any conversation with the telephonists sitting next to us. We had to clock on when we came on duty and if we were three minutes late, we had to work fifteen minutes extra at night. We had to wear black half-sleeves (you sometimes see us wearing them on old films). We also wore a big black apron with big pockets for pencils etc.

Boys took the telegrams out on bicycles. Some firms sent phonograms. They would ask for telegrams and we would write them down and phone them through.

The Paupers' Snuff

In the 1920s, after a cataract operation had forced him to leave his previous job, Mr Pass took over the newsagents and tobacconists shop on Sharrow Vale Road from his father. He was helped by his wife who, before her marriage, had been in service at Shirle Hill.

Their son Donald, now in his eighties, remembers how his mother was always dismayed by the rather strange appearance of the 'paupers' from the Union Workhouse when they came into the shop on Saturdays. "There used to be about twenty of them and they were let in two at a time. They'd come for their bags of snuff — a small scoop for a ha'penny and a large scoop for a penny — forty or fifty bags in all for themselves and their friends. The man who had the pork shop on Sharrow Vale Road used to give them a bit of black pudding. Everybody was very sorry for the paupers."

Donald Pass can also tell you about the days when he was soloist and head boy of the choir at St Andrew's. On Sunday mornings, before the service at the church, the choir would go up to the workhouse at nine o'clock to sing in the chapel there which was always full of plants and flowers brought by the well-off ladies of the area. "The paupers used to shuffle into the chapel. They didn't look too keen. The women always wore black shawls. Afterwards we were taken into the room next to the Master's office for a drink of milk. We'd heard that if we had this milk then the paupers wouldn't get any in their tea that day. Now that really upset me and I refused on behalf of the choir." However the Master, who Donald remembers as a very friendly and cheerful man ("not hard-hearted, as you might expect") told him that this story was not true and that the inmates would still have milk in their tea. So the choirboys accepted their drink!

The gates of Ecclesall Bierlow Union Workhouse must have clanged dismally behind many paupers as they entered the dreaded 'House'.

The Lantern Theatre

◆ **Mary Walton and Ruby McDonald**

The Lantern Theatre, Kenwood Park Road, during restoration.

There cannot be many suburban districts containing two fully-functioning theatres in which the amateur may practise his stagecraft. The Merlin is a modern, purpose-built theatre which is part of the Rudolph Steiner Centre in Tintagel House, comprising a school, the Merlin, classes for continuing education and the propagation of the views of the Anthroposophical Society. Briefly its history began with the St Philip's Settlement, a YMCA venture providing cultural and religious activities in Netherthorpe. It had as warden Arnold Freeman, who founded the St Philip's Settlement Dramatic Society, with its own Little Theatre in 1919. Although in 1923 many of the members left to found the Sheffield Repertory Company, Freeman continued to produce established classics in the Little Theatre; through various changes, the Sheffield Education Settlement, as it was renamed, came to place its emphasis on the Steiner philosophy. About 1960 the work of the settlement was transferred to Tintagel House, and in 1969 was provided with the Merlin Theatre. I hope that some day all this will be recorded in print.

But the story of the Lantern Theatre in Kenwood Park Road is entirely private and domestic.

In 1886 William Webster, a cutlery manufacturer, bought from Henry Stephenson a piece of land in Priory Road, with permission to build a house on it. This plan was carried out; over the doorway of No 40 Priory Road is the date 1889. In 1893 he bought the adjoining piece of land at the corner of

Priory Road and Kenwood Park Road, with permission to build a house and/or (it is not clear which) chalet or summer house; and almost immediately the chalet was built. I have not been able to sort out the truth from the various accounts current in the neighbourhood of this venture; some say that one of his daughters wanted to go on the stage, but that William, horrified (as many fathers were then) at the idea, built the nice little building so that she could play at acting. Others maintain stoutly that he had only one daughter, and this seems to be supported by the fact that only one is mentioned in the legal documents I have been allowed to consult. Was this, in fact, the stage-struck one? She was a member for many years of St Andrew's Church but among those now living who remember her, none ever heard her, or anyone else, say anything to suggest it.

William Webster died in 1895, and eventually his daughter, Florence May, was the only member of the family living in the house. He had left it to trustees (of whom Florence was one) with provisions about its disposal which are only partly quoted in the conveyance I have seen so that I do not exactly understand why, after Florence left for a smaller house,

Jack Hulbert opens the restored Lantern Theatre in 1957. Dilys Guite stands at the back beside Alderman Ballard, the Lord Mayor.

Before the Dilys Guite Players moved in . . .

. . . and the view from the stage after their work was completed.

No. 40 Priory Road remained virtually unused for years. From about 1920 to 1924 it was tenanted by Miss Mabel Jeye, who established in it a Sheffield School of Elocution and Dramatic Art, with what she named 'the Chalet Theatre' as a studio. I attended a performance myself in 1920 or 1921 with other members of my class at school; the production (it was Sophocles' Antigone, no less) had considerable merit. This lady was an active member of the Sheffield Playgoers' Society and produced some plays for them; but in the directory for 1924 the name of the school has disappeared, and so has Miss Jeye. I have failed to find anything more about her. Only caretakers appear in later directories.

In 1934 Florence and her fellow trustees conveyed the house and chalet to C. E. Richardson of Millthorpe near Holmesfield, and his wife.

Ruby McDonald now takes up the story:

For more than thirty years after Miss Jeye's time the theatre stood empty. Mr Richardson refused many tempting offers to buy it, living in the hope that one day someone would come along with the urge to restore and rebuild it as a theatre again.

Fortunately a local drama teacher, Dilys Guite, and her players did finally appear in the 1950s. After discussions he decided to rent the building to them for the vast sum of £1 a week. The auditorium at that time consisted of one large room with small tables and chairs, an open fireplace at one side and a raised stage at one end for the performers, but the place had become derelict during its long period of disuse.

The fantastic work of restoration, carried out mostly by the weary and concerted efforts of the Dilys Guite Players, can be seen in the photographs. Mr Richardson was so impressed that he decided to present the theatre to them as a free gift, a marvellous and much appreciated gesture.

So the Lantern Theatre came into being, renamed after the architectural feature on the roof. It was opened in 1957 by the well-known actor Jack Hulbert, with the Lord Mayor and Lady Mayoress and Dilys Guite herself, who produced 'The Dark Lady of the Sonnets' for the event. The opening production of the first season was 'The Merry Wives of Windsor'.

Although Dilys did not live to see her project come to full maturity, the Lantern Theatre is still flourishing. It now has refurbished dressing rooms and a new extension containing a coffee bar, and runs a costume hiring service which is proving very profitable. Theatrical productions of a very high standard are still being regularly produced there, as they have been for the last thirty years.

Changes at Sharrow Vale

◆ Margaret Andrews

Sharrow Vale, alongside the Porter Brook and therefore lower lying than its near neighbour, Nether Edge, was quite different from that prosperous and growing suburb in the middle of the nineteenth century. Here industry was well established with the two snuff mills and the Upper Lescar grinding wheel near Hunter's Bar and the Lower Lescar Wheel adjacent to the Porter Cottage public house. At the latter wheel Samuel Cocker & Sons made wire, pins, needles and fish hooks when they expanded in the 1830s and in 1865 a Charles Sanderson was cashing in on the current fashion making wire for crinoline hoops.

Around 1880 crowded living conditions in the area of The Moor probably caused the more enterprising artisans to think of moving further afield to better air and space for their families, yet still within easy walking distance of their place of work. From this time the Sharrow Vale area was developed for housing.

The first casualty seems to have been the Lower Lescar dam which was drained, automatically closing the works there, although the Upper Lescar dam still existed when the first Hunter's Bar Board School opened in 1893.

It is interesting to learn of some of the very local occupations of those who came to live on Sharrow Vale Road between 1883 and 1898. There was a shoemaker, two green grocers, three grocers, a confectioner and several 'shopkeepers' along with two butchers, one bearing the name Hogg which was to remain for over sixty years. An enterprising Miss Stuart appears to have started a steam laundry, apparently separate from the slightly later large concern, the Sharrow Vale Sanitary Steam Laundry, near Cowlishaw Road, which was owned by Thomas Watson and Co. Herbert Walker was a petroleum dealer in 1893.

To cater for very different needs came John Stokes, surgeon, at No 273 and Henry Spurgeon Fulston who combined his tailoring with the position of sub-postmaster at No 257 — a rare achievement? Perhaps his name helped!

Two Sheffield nurserymen seem to have started their well-known businesses at Sharrow Vale around this time. William Artindale operated somewhere not far from the present Hickmott Road and was also known as a seedsman and florist. Brooke Bray built himself a large double fronted house near Steel Road and a shop, with stabling extending round the corner. His nurseries near the top of Greystones Road served several retail outlets until taken for housing in the 1950s.

A smithy was built in 1888 between 275 and 277 Sharrow Vale Road and its first occupant was a Benjamin Lambert who had worked for a time on the opposite side of the road. A well-known blacksmith, Montague (Monty) Gilbert, took over in 1905, at twenty-one said to be the youngest smith in Sheffield. He possessed only a hammer and anvil and made himself a pair of tongs from a solid piece of iron, no mean feat. His four sons were born in the adjacent house. As well as shoeing horses, rims were made for wheels and it was not uncommon for as many as four horses and carts from farms and local businesses to be waiting outside the premises. Two sons carried on the business after their father's death in 1938 and it remained in operation, though on a decreasing scale, until the 1950s. The two hearths remained until around 1960 and the premises are now used by a saw manufacturer. Another smith worked on Lescar Lane for a time; Paddy 'Whisker' Eyres seems to have been something of a character, not adverse to dipping his false teeth in the 'bothy' water from time to time!

Alas, progress meant the end for George Ashton and the Sharrow Vale farm behind the Porter Cottage public house and presumably for Mrs Fanny Mather, cowkeeper, on Back Lane behind Monty Gilbert's smithy, as more houses were built. The beautiful horse trough, a crossing point for school children, was retired to a field off Common Lane when Hunter's Bar was widened and altered around 1963.

Sharrow Smithy, some time before the First World War. Albert Macrae stands at the anvil, and on the left is Joe Loosemore, elder brother of Arnold Loosemore VC.

Monty Gilbert photographed in the 1930s with his sons Colin, standing, and Fred, seated with the dog.

Tom Whittaker ◆ Jackie Hamilton

Tom Whittaker aged 17, with a Sopwith Dolphin at the pilot training school in Beaulieu, Hampshire, in 1917.

On 4th August 1914 Tom Whittaker was called to the front of his class at Walkley School and instructed by Mr Bott to read out the declaration of war printed in *The Times*. Shortly afterwards, he left school. He had applied for work with Thomas Firth but since they were rather slow at arranging the interview and it would have been considered a disgrace not to start work on the Monday after leaving school, his first job was with a dairy on Pinstone Street. The great attraction of this particular job was that one of the 'perks' was a bicycle which was also available for private use. As well as many journeys into the surrounding countryside, this bicycle enabled Tom to perform his first war service. This involved him in sleeping under the billiard tables at West Bar and Rockingham Street fire stations. Many firemen did not live on the premises and, since they did not have telephones, when a Zeppelin raid was anticipated out would go Tom and his friend to raise the alarm.

This job provided further excitement in an encounter with Sarah Bernhardt. The actress was staying at the Grand Hotel and insisted on milk being specially delivered to her suite. In a huge bed, swathed in satin and lace, she received visitors. She pronounced Tom 'un joli garçon' and he was much gratified by her heavily accented command to her maid to 'give him a shilling'.

In July 1917 Major Lord Howick's Examination Board was at the Corn Exchange looking for recruits for cadets for the Royal Flying Corps. The first question was always 'can you ride a horse?' The majority of pilots were from the cavalry and both skills were considered to be a matter of having good hands. Whatever the then powers-that-be thought, Tom Whittaker has another theory. Those he considers the very best of the Great War pilots, Captain Ball, Major McCudden and Major Mannock, all VCs, had all been professional cyclists. Although the Board queried his riding ability they never asked his age and so, at sixteen years and six feet tall, Tom Whittaker joined the Royal Flying Corps. After training at Farnborough and Beaulieu in Avro 504Ks and Dolphins, and with a total of nine and a half hours flying time, he was posted to France, first to 201 Squadron flying Sopwith Camels and then to 204 Squadron; the latter move when the squadron had lost nine out of fifteen pilots in one day. Strafing raids and dogfights were exciting but frequently deadly and the life of a pilot was often counted in days and weeks rather than months. However, on 11th November 1918 came the armistice and a week later Second Lieut. Whittaker was eighteen!

The Royal Flying Corps became the Royal Air Force in 1918 and Tom Whittaker stayed in the service until 1920, in

Southern Arabia and in Egypt where he met General Allenby whom he found to be most friendly and charming.

After leaving the RAF he went to Sheffield University, on an engineering course. Eventually he worked for Newton Chambers and then for Shell-Mex for many years.

As a boy Tom had been a keen Scout, learning many of the skills such as map reading and signalling which were to stand him in such good stead during his flying days. As soon as he was discharged he went back to his old troop and was soon asked to become Scoutmaster. However, Wolf Cubs had just been introduced and he elected to become Cubmaster and formed a troop. He led these boys on many excursions, frequently returning via Rivelin Valley Road past the King Edward VII Hospital. At this time the hospital was for crippled children and, after visiting with his Rover Scouts many times, permission was given to establish the 148th Sheffield, the first troop in the world for crippled boys.

When the Whittakers moved to High Green he had to leave the 148th but became Cubmaster with 3rd Wentworth and eventually founded the High Green troop in May 1926. In 1986 he proudly took the salute when they celebrated sixty years of Scouting in High Green.

Another interest from those days was amateur dramatics. With the Chapeltown Society, Shell-Mex Group and eventually The Sheffield Playgoers both Mr Whittaker and his wife were devoted members; acting, producing, making costumes and some memorable scenery. His theatrical experience was of great value when, after the Second World War, Tom Whittaker produced the Annual Festival of Remembrance at the City Hall. He did this for eleven years until the cost of hiring the Hall became prohibitive and the Festival was abandoned. On one occasion seventy units marched on to the platform, many with regimental standards. Major Jubb, Bandmaster of the Signals Regiment, congratulated the producer on what must have been 'many months of rehearsal'. When he discovered that the precision was the result of detailed planning but only half an hour of actual rehearsal, he was astonished.

Tom Whittaker maintained a keen interest in service life. He joined the Fellowship of the Services in 1934 and became National Chairman in 1968. He was commanding officer of the 367 Squadron Air Training Corps in the Second World War and was still much in demand to attend ceremonies and to speak at these and many other associations and groups of which he had been a member and in many cases helped to found, until his death a few months ago.

Laurence Mullins
◆ Joan Oldfield and Betty and Harold Howe

Laurence Mullins, better known as Lol or Bob, was an institution in Nether Edge. His father had been Clerk of Works at the Ecclesall Bierlow Union Workhouse, so young Laurence had frequented the area from childhood. As a boy he learnt many of his skills at the Workhouse. He mixed paints and did building repairs alongside his father, learnt much of the undertaker's trade and repaired shoes as well as being entrusted with errands for the doctors.

Although he won a scholarship to King Edward VII School Laurence Mullins preferred to continue at elementary school and leave at fourteen to become a wage earner. He did, however, attend evening classes in art and some of his drawings of leaves were so lifelike that they looked as if they could be picked up. In the last ten years of his life, after his wife's death, he returned to art classes and produced some very interesting pictures.

In the Second World War he joined the Royal Air Force, although he had sustained so many broken bones in his early working life that it was amazing he was accepted as a recruit. He rose through the ranks to Warrant Officer, and would have liked to make the Air Force his career. However, his wife preferred life at 2 Oakdale Road to the prospect of RAF married quarters, so Laurence Mullins came back to his property repairing and decorating business in Nether Edge.

He was a mine of information about the Victorian properties in the area, many of which have benefited from his repairs, and he could recognise the quarries from which their building stones had come.

He bred both canaries and mice, and went around the country judging them at shows. There was a time when he supplied mice of his own breeding to the University. He was a keen gardener and many of us have plants in our gardens grown from seed which he harvested in his own.

Whatever Laurence Mullins turned his hand to, he did well — tailoring, knitting, baking, carpentry, photography (tinting photographs with great delicacy when this process was fashionable) watch repairing and, during his RAF days, making tiny model aeroplanes with great precision. The accounts he kept for his business were meticulous, everything being itemised in a beautiful hand. He was always glad to pass on his wide knowledge and expertise.

Laurence Mullins in his RAF days.

Betty Howe remembers: Mr Mullins was very fond of children. He hid this carefully under a stern and rather gruff exterior, which brought out the best in the young — they responded by behaving well and being stimulated to interest in his stories and information.

Whilst working in my house in Edgehill Road he offered to keep an eye on my nine year old daughter, who was ill with measles, so I could go shopping. On my return I was amazed at the felt toy she showed me. She was (and still is) an inept needlewoman and had struggled painfully for days to complete the object. When I exclaimed at the perfect stitches the reply was 'Mr Mullins finished it for me!'

A seemingly forbidding manner concealed an impish and at times Rabelaisian sense of humour. He would never reveal whether the escape of live rats from a sack he was once carrying in this boyhood on the Meadowhead tram was deliberate, and his account of clearing blocked drains was not for the squeamish.

Laurence Mullins retired at sixty-five to care for his sick wife, but at seventy-nine he was still climbing on to his roof to help and instruct his grandson in its repair.

For an active man of such wide gifts and achievements, his last years of failing powers nust have proved particularly irksome. However he was always courageous and showed, perhaps more clearly than in former times, an innate ability to laugh at himself. He added character to Nether Edge, and since his death at eighty-one in April 1988 Oakdale Road will never be quite the same again.

Leslie Perkins De Abrew

MRCS (England), LRCP (London) ◆ Joan Oldfield

The ship bearing Leslie Perkins de Abrew from Colombo to France en route to England was shadowed by a U-boat. It was World War I. He was never to return to his native country although his father had hoped that he would join his medical practice there.

Dr de Abrew was born in Ceylon, now Sri Lanka, in 1882, probably in Colombo. He started his medical career there and came to the London Hospital to complete it. He graduated in London in 1917.

His first medical appointment appears to have been that of ophthalmic and aural house surgeon and house surgeon at the Royal Hospital, West Street, Sheffield. He was then appointed temporary Assistant Medical Officer at the Ecclesall Institution, Nether Edge, formerly the Ecclesall Bierlow Union Workhouse, on 15th February 1919. The position was made permanent on 18th February 1920 at a salary of £300 and, as War Bonuses were still being paid, this salary was supplemented by £70. According to the minutes of the Ecclesall Bierlow Union for 14th April 1920, sanction was received for the appointment of Dr de Abrew as Resident Medical Officer of the Ecclesall Institution and for the residence of his wife at the Institution. His wife, a Scot, had been a nursing sister at the Royal Hospital.

In 1921 Dr de Abrew's salary was fixed at £300 per annum plus £100 emoluments and £85 War Bonus. His wife's rations were fixed at £50 per annum. In March 1926 the family, which now included a small daughter, Isobel, moved to 38 Edgehill Road and the doctor's salary was increased to £625 per annum. His War Bonus ceased on 1st April that year.

At a Board meeting on 30th March 1927 it was stated that the Ministry of Health had approved the proposal that Dr de Abrew should act as House Surgeon for the Maternity Department of the Institution on the assumption that he would not carry septic or infected cases elsewhere. It has to be remembered that, at that time, there were wards of chronic tuberculosis cases at the Institution.

In 1929 the Institution became known as Nether Edge Hospital and came under the management of the Corporation of the City of Sheffield under the direction of a Medical Superintendent. Dr de Abrew was appointed Medical Superintendent on 29th August 1945, and as Obstetrician Superintendent on 1st October 1949. His contract as whole-time Senior Medical Officer, outlined in a letter from the

Dr de Abrew in his garden at Edgehill Road.

Sheffield Regional Hospital Board of 21st December 1950, was back-dated to 1st October 1949. His duties, detailed in a document dated 6th November 1952, were:
1. On call for all emergencies, night and day.
2. Examination of new entrants to nursing and other posts.
3. Medical care of nursing and domestic sick.
4. Any matter of a medical administrative nature.

Ward rounds, along with one other doctor, occupied from six to eight hours daily. There were ante-natal and post-natal sessions each week and operating sessions on the labour ward when necessary. There had been a period when the operating theatre at the hospital had been closed and this had been a great sadness to Dr de Abrew when he had been unable to perform necessary Caesarian sections. He was dedicated to his patients and he did a ward round every day, even on his weekends off duty. He did, however, play tennis on the courts at the Hospital. He had also played cricket in Ceylon and maintained a spectator interest in it all his life.

In March 1950, as part of the post-war plans, a new maternity unit was opened by the Lord Mayor, Mrs Grace Tebbutt. The unit had cost £45,000 and, at the opening ceremony, it was noted that when the previous maternity unit was opened in 1927, 239 confinements took place in a year compared with the 1947 peak of 932. In an article entitled 'The New Maternity Unit at Nether Edge Hospital, Sheffield' in the *Hospital and Social Services Journal* for April 1950 it was stated that the new unit would be of great benefit. In the nine years prior to 1950 there had been only three deaths in all the mothers who had been patients at the Hospital, a tribute to the skills and abilities of the nurses and staff. Dr de Abrew was always involved in the fight for funds to improve the Hospital including those which resulted, after his retirement, in the developments in 1967 to 1970.

On 10th March 1957, Leslie Perkins de Abrew ceased full-time duties at Nether Edge Hospital but from 11th March 1957 undertook part-time duties for four notional half days a week. A luncheon was held in his honour in May 1958 when he was presented with a television set costing £52 0s. 4d. The total cost of the provisions for the occasion was £3 5s. 0d.! He retired from all duties at the Hospital in July 1958. *The Star* for 7th March 1958 had the headline 'Doctor ends 40 years work in hospitals'. 'Dr de Abrew was the longest serving member on the staff of Nether Edge Hospital'. He was quoted as saying, 'I came to this country intending to stay a short time, then somebody asked me to stay on. I have been so long here that I consider myself one of you. I have always been happy here. I will always remember the extreme heroism of the nursing staff and porters during the Blitz in 1940. They were wonderful.' This was a reference to December 1940 when a wall was blown out of a maternity ward during an air raid. A nurse pushed one patient under her bed and a doctor and nurse delivered the baby under the bed.

After his retirement Dr de Abrew worked as a part-time practitioner at the Mother and Child Welfare Clinic in Orchard Street, Sheffield, in spite of failing eyesight. Dr Flowerday, a colleague at the clinic, said of him, 'He was an excellent medical practitioner, remarkably kind to his patients, who adored him. A man who knew his limitations and worked neither beyond his training nor his capacity — an attribute exceptional within his profession. Handicapped by his lack of vision, he was slow and it was necessary for letters and notes concerning his patients to be read to him. He was appreciative of the thoughtfulness of others and easy to co-operate with as a medical partner.'

Dr de Abrew died at his home in Edgehill Road in 1978. He had continued his work at the Mother and Child Welfare Clinic until a few years before his death and to this day his widow, Marion, and daughter are surprised and pleased by the praise expressed at the mention of the name de Abrew. Women met by chance praise him and pronounce the doctor who attended them in childbirth 'a gentleman'. It is obvious that Dr de Abrew devoted his life to his patients and had no thought for accolade.

First School Days ◆ Jimmi Eldridge

Peardrops and aniseed bring instant memories of my first day at school. It was 1937 and the place was a house at the junction of Archer Lane and Bannerdale Road in which Miss Meays held her Infant school. The first hours seemed like forever, and then a bell rang and we were all ushered into a room with a large dark brown cupboard and a table on which there was a small set of weighing scales. Beside the scales stood two large glass stoppered jars and a pile of cone shaped paper bags. The glass stoppers were removed and instantly the air was filled with the delightful smell of peardrops and aniseed. A child stepped forward and proffered a farthing and with a great ritual a small scoopful of the sweets was poured into a cone of paper and carefully weighed on the scales. A new word entered my vocabulary . . . Tuckshop! But I was unprepared, no farthing clutched in my hand! A short consultation between the adults ensued and I was allowed a coneful of the sweets, on the strict understanding that payment would be forthcoming the following day. Needless to say, I was never unprepared again.

Shortly afterwards the school moved to a larger house at the junction of Bannerdale Road and Carterknowle Road. Here there was much more space and a larger area outside in which to play at recreation time. The time spent here was a jumbled memory of the dreaded annual Hovis Art competition, for which everyone had to submit an original piece of art work, and hope desperately that it would be chosen and forwarded to what sounded like a great loaf in the sky. The library, which consisted of two shelves of assorted books . . . Here one could borrow a book to read during recreation time. The delight of this was twofold. The excitement of a new subject to be discovered each day and the condition that the book could only be read indoors. In bad weather this last was a boon. While everyone else donned wellies and macs and stoically plodded out into the playground, the readers were perforce snug and smug indoors! I became an avid reader. I also dimly remember that sometimes we used small slates for what was termed rough work and then later transferred the work onto paper.

Came the war. The school was transferred to the Manor House on Oakdale Road. Here we revelled in having our lessons in the Edwardian luxury of the conservatory. But this delightful venue was terminated by the Blitz when the glass was shattered and the building was no longer habitable.

When normality returned I became a pupil at Lynwood Mount on Moncrieffe Road. This school was much larger. It was organised by the Misses Sanderson — two genteel ladies of indeterminate age. They wore identical suits of Dove Grey knitted silk and were never seen to wear anything but these suits. We used to conjecture whether it was the same two suits or whether they had, indeed, several identical ones! The senior Miss Sanderson was the Headmistress, she was tall and slender and graceful. Her sister was less fortunate, being short, plump and a trifle hirsute. Sad to relate, we always referred to them as Fatty and Thinny.

The Manor House, built in the 1850s on the site of Upper Edge farm, was photographed in about 1875 by Theophilus Smith. More recently it was used as a school until damaged in the Blitz.

The school was very well organised. In retrospect, I realize that the Misses Sanderson worked exceedingly hard. They had two junior assistants but they themselves taught all the major subjects to everyone. The juniors were only present to oversee our work when we were left to write up on the subject in hand.

Apart from a very thorough grounding in all the traditional subjects, we were constantly reminded that we were the children of a sovereign and mighty empire. Every major campaign and historic event was ritually remembered on the relevant day of the year. Prayers for the Royal family, the fighting forces, the Empire and Commonwealth, Missionaries in the field of Moral Conflict and a host of other worthy causes were all dutifully remembered in daily assembly.

At this school I stayed for lunch each day. This was organised by a large motherly lady. It commenced with a square of Yorkshire Pudding and gravy, followed by a simple but filling main course and terminated by an even more filling steamed pudding and custard. It was consistently the same every day. But I do not recall that we ever complained at the monotony. Once a week we went into the gym. This was a large room over the stable block and had previously been the Billiard Room. Here we had Musical Exercise. I now realise that this was actually directly influenced by Isadora Duncan. Fatty played the piano, painstakingly. Thinny demonstrated and instructed us in movements and classical poses in unison with the music. This was the only class in the week that was for girls only. The boys had craft lessons while we danced, undoubtedly because it would have been unthinkable that they should see us cavorting in just our blouses and thick woolly knickers, having abandoned our skirts for greater freedom of movement. My dread of the week was singing class. To be unable to sing was tantamount to having a physical disability in the eyes of the Misses Sanderson. I was acutely disabled.

Apart . . . we were instructed in French, Music and Botany, this last being taught with the aid of several beautifully illustrated old Botany books that had belonged to Papa Sanderson. Similarly, needlework was instructed via the use of the books and delicate samples that had been the property of Mama Sanderson.

We all had a profound respect for the softly spoken, firm but gentle, elder Miss Sanderson. Alas, we were not so understanding of the younger and must have tormented her many times. Sadly, I now realise that these dauntless ladies, who devoted their lives to instilling their knowledge, skills and unshakable moral values into us, belonged to that 'lost' generation for whom the satisfaction of creating and raising their own children and been denied by the sacrifices of War. I would have liked to have told them that their reward was that we gained immeasurably by their loss.

Wilf Green

Motor Cycle Dealer   ◆ Malcolm Weston

To a pimply youth in the late 1940s, Wilf Green's motor cycle shop a few doors away from the Abbeydale Cinema (and still a motor cycle shop) demanded a weekly visit. Not that we could actually afford anything more lavish than a push-bike — but we could dream!

Most Sunday afternoons we would start at Roper's motor cycle shop on London Road and then progress to Dan Bradbury's also on London Road. Horridge and Wildgoose, the Triumph agents on Highfields, were the next drooling stop and then the long hike up Abbeydale Road to Wilf Green's was made less tedious by the thought of a refreshing hot Vimto in Pop's Temperance Bar (now, of course, an 'antique' shop). By way of a change we'd walk the other way the following Sunday!

Wilf was born in Thirlwell Road, Abbeydale, in 1914 and attended Carterknowle and Abbeydale schools. He passed the 'Scholarship' exam for Grammar School but, like so many others, he was unable to take advantage of the opportunity owing to the cost of the uniform, etc.

Starting work at fourteen, he worked part-time as a delivery boy for Mair's the bakers on Ecclesall Road but his mechanical interest soon led him to a job at Shardlow Engineering as a crankshaft grinder. (At a recent open day he was amused to see that a couple of machines which he operated in the 1930s were still in daily use — a testimony to the lack of investment in British Industry!)

Being very interested in motor cycles he started doing back yard repairs, his very first customer being a Mr Hawley (of Hawley Tyres) who lived on Crescent Road. His 1931 174cc Triumph was fitted with a novelty which Mr Hawley was making at the time. This was the 'Hawley Buoy Pillion Seat' — a sort of blow up cushion fitted over the rear mudguard.

The shed at the rear of Thirlwell Road was soon outgrown and Wilf rented a row of garages in Salmon Street (off Club Garden Road), still as a part-time venture.

When war came along he serviced the motor cycles used by the ARP and Fire Service until these organisations built their own facilities; additionally he was reconditioning all the vehicles belonging to Turner & Co (the tyre guage people who later became Pneumatic Components Ltd, now part of the Rio Tinto group).

As he was still working full time at Shardlows in addition to being a member of the Auxiliary Fire Service it became obvious that Wilf was, and is, a 'grafter' who would have succeeded in any line of business.

Wilf Green and canine friend at Mallory Park circuit.

Wilf in action at a 1949 grass track meeting.

As the war was drawing to a close he rented a shop at Abbeydale Road (still a motor cycle shop) for the full-time repair and sale of second-hand machines but with the ultimate aim of getting a dealership for one of the leading makes.

This was a daunting task as the trade in Sheffield was cosily controlled by the long established dealers such as Ropers, Bradburys, Wraggs etc, who had no which to see a new, young and vigorous upstart upsetting the applecart whilst the manufacturers had a vested interest in supporting the 'establishment' against all comers.

As direct approaches had met with a blank wall of indifference Wilf embarked on a lengthy and persistent process of guile, subterfuge and coercion which eventually led to Royal Enfield offering him a spare parts dealership. This was the first toe-hold to official recognition that he'd been seeking and he was able to use it as a lever to open many of the doors which had been firmly closed against him.

The irony is that twenty years later, as the Japanese bike invasion got underway, many of these same makers were knocking on his door begging for orders!

As he could see that the British Motor Cycle Industry was on its last legs in the early 1970s he looked around the world for suitable machines and eventually settled on the East German MZ range of motor cycles as an alternative to going Japanese. So successful was this decision that he has gradually become the sole importer for the UK and supplies about 250 dealers throughout the country.

Now in his seventies he still retains great vigour and a zest for life. The day before our talk he had ridden over 200 miles on his old Norton and thoroughly enjoyed it. He lives in his splendid Victorian house in the Kenwood area where he has lived for thirty years surrounded by his beloved vintage motor cycles and the memorabilia of an eventful life. He still works for two or three days a week — 'Just to keep an eye on the petty cash!'

The original Abbeydale Road shop in the 1940s, prior to extensions.

Memories of Nether Edge in the 1940 Blitz ◆ Collected by Shirley Meek

I have a personal interest in the stories that follow. Although I was a long way from Sheffield that night, as a thirteen year old schoolgirl I watched the city burn.

The sirens had gone early in the evening in Harrogate. We all went downstairs but as usual nothing seemed to be happening in our district. When the All Clear went around midnight I climbed up to my bedroom on the top floor of the house and looked out. A huge red flickering glow lit the sky to the south. "They must have got it badly in Leeds" we said. It was not until the next day that we discovered the truth: what we had seen was not Leeds but Sheffield burning, fifty miles distant from Harrogate. I have never forgotten that awe-inspiring vision of destruction.

Here are the recollections of some people who were in Nether Edge on that night of Thursday 12th December 1940. It was a brilliantly clear and frosty moonlit night, they all say, so bright that you could almost see to read a book outside. A perfect night for the raiders. . . .

MRS EVA JARMAN was expecting her second baby and, because her husband's school had been evacuated from West Ham in London to Bicester, she had come back to Sheffield to stay with her parents. She remembers:

That afternoon I had taken my son John, aged 21 months, to tea with an old school friend of mine who lived in Millhouses. It was a cold, bright winter's day, and I clearly remember walking up Sheldon Road in the dusk.

We lived at Cherry Tree Cottage, 11 Union Road, on the corner of Osborne Road. Before we lived there the house had been a butcher's shop, and there were three good cellars, two of which had stone tables for salting the meat. My father, who was Clerk of Works at Tennant Bros. Brewery, had had one of the cellars converted into an air raid shelter with four bunk beds and a space between for the baby's cot. There was an emergency exit through the coal cellar grate.

After putting John to bed in the shelter I settled down to do some sewing for the expected baby. Just after seven o'clock the sirens went and my parents, my aunt and I all went down to the cellar. Then enemy planes started dropping flares. My father went to the front door and an air raid warden shouted "If you've got a shelter, stay in it!" We heard planes overhead and the sound of bombs falling got nearer. Then the electricity failed and we had to rely on torches. My little boy was awake and standing up in his cot. Every time a bomb dropped he said "Bang!"

The bombs were getting closer and closer. One, a landmine, fell at the bottom of Lyndhurst Road, but the nearest was only a few yards away in Machon Bank Road where all the Pearson family was killed. A bomb fell on Nether Edge Hospital and patients were overcome with the fumes and the dust. There was a public air raid shelter in the Hospital grounds, and several local people took cover there.

We sat huddled together on our bunk beds and now and again my father looked out of the cellar grating. We never slept that night.

When the All Clear finally sounded we came up to assess the damage. The shelves at the cellar head had fallen down and the steps were covered with broken eggs, pots of jam and treacle. All thirteen windows in the house were broken and the debris from the bombed house nearby littered the back yard. Not realising at first how bad things were my mother went hopefully upstairs with a dustpan and brush! But she did find, and rescue, a cut glass candlestick which was just about to roll off the dressing table.

My father made arrangements to have the windows covered up, and then went off to walk to work at the Ladybridge Brewery. I hurried down to Rupert Road, where another aunt lived, and saw the devastation and burnt houses opposite her home. My aunt and uncle and a cousin were safe though, and they walked all the way to Dronfield to stay with friends. We went to stay with friends in Gisborne Road, Ecclesall.

When my husband heard on the radio that Sheffield had been bombed he came straight up to see what had happened, but it was some time before he could find where we had gone. We were all lucky to be alive!

(. . . but only those who have lived through food rationing will really appreciate the poignancy of the loss of those eggs and jam and treacle . . . SM)

Barrage balloon flying at Psalter Lane Methodist Church.

Devastation caused by the big bomb which fell in Kenwood Road.

A short way up Osborne Road, at No 76 **MRS RUBY McDONALD** had put her five year old daughter Jemima, or Jimmi, to bed at half past six in the dining room on the ground floor of the house. Her husband, who was manager of the Intake Cinema, was at work on the other side of the city.

The sirens went at 7.00 pm, and soon afterwards the first flares began to drop on Osborne Road. Mrs McDonald took Jimmi down to the cellar and then went next door to fetch the old lady and her daughter who were on their own there. The McDonalds' cats and bulldog shared the shelter too.

Incendiary bombs were now dropping all round, and from time to time Mrs McDonald came up from the cellar to see what was happening. About 9.00 pm she went upstairs and opened the attic door to find a large hole in the roof through which she could see straight up to the sky. A petrol bomb had fallen on the house and it was already burning. She knew that there was no time to be lost in getting the others out and hurried downstairs to take Jimmi and her neighbours to the public shelter in the hospital grounds.

The old lady, however, was most unwilling to move from the cellar into the fury of the raid outside. While they were arguing with her, and the house was burning over their heads, a soldier suddenly appeared. He had been passing by, had seen the flames and had come to see if anyone was trapped. He offered to carry the old lady to the shelter but she indignantly refused the offer and agreed to walk instead. So the party made its way down Osborne Road, through the flames and the hail of shrapnel. The cats disappeared but the bulldog caused further delay by getting entangled in the telephone wires which had been blown down and were festooning the road.

They all got to the shelter safely and took refuge under the solid buildings of the old Workhouse at the corner of Osborne Road and Union Road. It was a good thing that they had been so well constructed. When the landmine dropped at the junction of Lyndhurst and Union Roads Mrs McDonald remembers vividly how the thick stone walls shook around them. Mercifully this landmine fell in the middle of the road; if it had hit the hospital, a few yards away, there would have been a far greater loss of life.

They stayed in the shelter until the All Clear went in the early morning. Then they came out to find their house had been burnt to the ground. Mrs McDonald and Jimmi were taken in by a neighbour, Mrs Beard, at No 70 which was still standing. The family had to move into a rented house on Rundle Road for the rest of the war years, but after the war ended No 76 was completely rebuilt and Mrs McDonald is still living there today.

Not everyone's experiences were so dramatic. Round the corner at 41 St Andrew's Road **MR PETER FROST** and his mother and father were far luckier. He remembers going down to the cellar when the sirens sounded and having to stay there, though his father kept going up to see what was happening and report to the family. Fires were started at the hospital by the first wave of incendiary bombs, and the coal stores caught fire and blazed for a long time. The water mains had been cut and the water for the fire engines fighting the blaze had to be brought all the way from the river at Sharrow Vale in tenders. The Frosts could see Mrs McDonald's house burning and the old house at the corner of Cherry Tree Road and Meadow Bank Road was also alight.

Incendiaries dropped all round their garden but none fell on their house. They were far enough from the Lyndhurst Road landmine and the huge bomb which fell on Kenwood Road to escape the blast and, incredibly, not one of the Frosts' windows was broken.

Next day life was far from easy, even though they had escaped damage in the raid. Mr Frost's father had to walk all the way to his works in Saville Street across the shattered city. There was no electricity, no gas and no water; Mr Frost remembers getting water for cleaning up from a bomb crater outside the hospital. Drinking water supplies were brought round in a cart, and it was about ten days before the services were restored.

He also remembers certain neighbours who were so alarmed by the Blitz that they left next day for Derbyshire and were not seen again!

MRS FROST (senior), who is now 100 years old, has clear and vivid memories of an earlier raid on Sheffield. She lived in Edgedale Road during the First World War and one night she was coming back by rail from Rotherham when a Zeppelin, on its way to bomb Sheffield, actually followed the train overhead. The pilot must have been using the glow from the engine to guide the airship through the dark towards the city.

Coming back to 1940, **MR RONALD WILSON** was then a young man of eighteen, living at home with his mother and father at 12 Rundle Road. Mr Wilson senior had turned their cellar into a shelter by strengthening the living room floor, putting shutters on the windows and cutting an emergency exit. On the night of the Blitz Mr Ronald Wilson very clearly recalls the hooting of the owls in the early evening. There have always been owls in the Kenwood grounds, but this night they were hooting frantically; did they have some premonition?

The sirens went and the Wilsons went down to the shelter. When the first wave of incendiaries had dropped father and son went out to have a look. The bottom part of Kenbourne Road was well alight and a bomb was blazing away in the garden of No 10 Rundle Road, which belonged to John Mansell Jenkinson, the architect. Ronald Wilson jumped over the fence with a spade in his hand, shovelled earth on to the bomb and soon put that one out.

The second wave of planes brought the high explosive bombs. The most terrifying was the enormous bomb which fell in Kenwood Road, close to the present entrance of the Hotel St George. Mr Wilson remembers the whistle of that bomb as it came down getting louder and louder and louder . . . and when the explosion finally came, he says, the whole house lifted around them and his father rose several inches in the air. They were unhurt, though shocked, unlike the Homer family who lived at 52 Kenwood Park Road at the corner of Sharrow View. Their house was completely wrecked by another bomb, and the Homers' daughter was killed.

In the midst of all the noise and confusion the Wilsons heard someone running up their drive. It was a soldier, caught by the raid on his way back to the Army vehicle post up Lyndhurst Road. They gave him shelter for a while until a lull in the bombing allowed him to make another run for it.

Just before the All Clear, when everything seemed quiet again, a small delayed-action bomb exploded in the middle of Rundle Road near Rundle Drive. When it was light enough to see Mr Wilson walked round the corner to see what had happened in Kenwood Road. No 38 was completely demolished and No 40 was very badly damaged. Five trees in Kenwood Road had totally disappeared (and you can see the gap to this day) but they seemed to have taken the blast on that

The wardens of Mr Neville's post, photographed at Clifford School. Back Row: Mr Woollen, Mr Lockwood, Mr Neville, Mr Jackson, Mr Ansdell, Mr Warren, Mr McCallum. Front Row: Mr Lambert, Mrs Harland, Mr and Mrs Gibson, Mr Partridge, Mrs Woollen, Mr Beardshaw.

side and the Kenwood Hotel itself was not much affected. The crater left by the bomb was awe-inspiring. It was about 100 feet across and the spoil heap was 20 feet high. He climbed on top of the rubble and as he stood there he heard something ticking. Was it an unexploded bomb? No; when he kicked the earth to one side he found that it was the time clock from a street lamp which was still more or less upright but had been completely covered by debris from the explosion.

Ordinary people were in great danger, but at least they could stay in cellars or shelters under some sort of cover. The Air Raid Wardens, the Fire Service crews, the Ambulance drivers and the Messengers were outside all night in the thick of it. Here are the memories of two local Wardens:

MR KEN NEVILLE was living at 38 Psalter Lane when war broke out in September 1939. He was turned down by the Army, so he became an Air Raid Warden. His Post was in the cellars of 30 Psalter Lane which belonged to one of the Harland brothers who owned the Top Snuff Mill. Mr Gibson, of Rundle Road, was the Chief Warden.

Some Wardens were on duty each night, two from 7.00 to 10.00 pm and four from 10.00 pm to 6.00 am. These four worked shifts of two hours on and two hours off, and they could sleep at the Post when they were off shift. They had to walk round the neighbourhood to check that the blackout was complete and no lights were showing. The area they covered was from Sharrow Vale Road to Kenwood Road and back to Cowlishaw Road, including Clifford Road and Psalter Lane. They also had to call at every house regularly to note who was living there and to record their next of kin in case of death or injury in a raid.

Of course when the sirens went all the Wardens had to report at their Post and stay there until the All Clear sounded. There had been dozens of warnings in the autumn of 1940, especially on the nights when the German planes flew over to raid Liverpool, but few incidents in Sheffield until the evening of 12th December. Mr Neville was on his way to night school at Hunters Bar when the sirens sounded and he had to dash back to his Post. Within half an hour of the alarm incendiaries were dropping and many fires had been started. One of the biggest blazes was at Westbrook Bank. The Wardens were trying to deal with the fire when they heard a bomb coming down. They ran for their lives to the shelter of a passage way between the houses and fell flat. Fortunately they chose the upper side of the street. If they had run for the opposite passage Mr Neville would not have been alive to tell me his story, because that was where the bomb landed.

Several people were injured in the explosion. When the rescue squad arrived to get them out, a soldier was found trapped in the cellar. They started to dig him out by the light of the blazing house next door. Some time later a mobile First Aid party and an ambulance arrived from Greystones Ambulance Station. There was a widely held belief that bombs, like lightning, never struck the same place twice; but at midnight another high explosive bomb did hit almost exactly the same spot and buried the men of the rescue squad, the ambulance driver and some of the First Aid party under the ruins. One man got out and went back to Greystones to get volunteers, who were joined by an Army rescue unit. It was not until half past four that they got to the victims. By then the leader of the First Aid party and the ambulance driver were dead, together with three of the original rescue squad. The rest were badly injured and there were casualties among civilians too. The injured were treated on a mattress which had been blown out of the ruins, while neighbours brought blankets and hot drinks. Then the new rescue squad went back to the trapped soldier who was, incredibly, still alive. They fought to free him for forty hours, but when they finally did release him he died from his injuries in hospital.

Of all the other incidents in his area that night, the one that Mr Neville remembers most vividly came after he had been sent to Bowood Road to put out another fire. He was on his way back up Bagshot Street when he heard the whistle of a

falling bomb and threw himself down under a wall for shelter. As he turned his head he saw the nearby lamp post disintegrating in front of his eyes; a moment later there was nothing left to show where it had stood.

One very interesting memory from much later in the War is of seeing 'buzz bombs' or V1s pass over Sheffield, going out to the west. Few people realise that these weapons ever came as far north as Sheffield but I have spoken to several other people who also remember seeing them.

On the other side of Nether Edge MR FRANK TEMBEY was the Chief Warden of the Post at Abbeydale School on Glen Road. At that time he was living as 43 Oakhill Road with his wife and his mother and he had joined up as an Air Raid Warden some months before the Was started, training with the police.

His Post was in the cellars under the school. The area covered was from Abbeydale Road to Union Road and from Sheldon Road to Brincliffe Edge. There were eight or nine Wardens in all, including three women, and on that Thursday night they were really tested. Hundreds of people came to shelter in the school, some in the cellars and some just hoping that the solid walls would give them protection above ground. Bombs fell all over the neighbourhood, from the very beginning of the raid to the end. One of the biggest fell in Abbeydale Road in front of the school, between Glen Road and Marden Road. It left a huge crater and broke the culvert which carries the Edge Brook down to the Sheaf. MR DONALD PASS was in the Home Guard and he remembers helping to direct the traffic around the flood after walking back through the Blitz from Crookes.

In spite of all they went through that night none of the Wardens was injured, but many casualties were brought into the Post for treatment and first aid. One man was obviously in a very serious condition but as the telephone lines had been cut early in the evening there was no way of calling an ambulance. Mr Tembey volunteered to go on foot to the Southern District headquarters in Chelsea Road in the hope that their phones might still be working. He went by way of Brincliffe Edge Road and called in at a house where he knew his wife and mother would be sheltering. Here a man who had been in the Army offered to come with him. On their way along Brincliffe Edge Mr Tembey heard a strange new noise, a popping sound. He was puzzled as to what it could be but the soldier knew well enough. They were being machine gunned.

They got to Chelsea Road HQ safely, having survived both the machine gunners and the landmine which fell on Lyndhurst Road when they were only a short distance away, and found the phones were still working. Mr Tembey simply comments "It was amazing how quickly you got used to the bombs".

There were too many incidents to recount them all. In Rupert Road there was serious damage, with several houses on fire. In Oakhill Road No 33 was flattened, but mercifully the Belton family was in the cellar of the house next door and so escaped. Oakdale Road had what might have been the most devastating incident of the lot: a huge landmine came down by parachute into the grounds of No 25 but it failed to explode. It remained there, half in and half out of the ground, at the corner of Adelaide Road. Next day the whole area was evacuated, as far away as Nether Edge Road and Violet Bank Road. The residents were sent to Carterknowle School, where they had to live for several days while the Army Bomb Disposal Unit dug out and defused the monster. Their Captain told Mr Tembey that if the mine had gone off it would have cleared everything within a quarter mile radius. It was later put on show in Fargate to collect funds for charity. The old house at No 25 survived the Blitz only to fall victim to developers twenty years later, and a block of flats stands there today.

Although Oakhill Road had been evacuated and was officially closed at both top and bottom, Mr and Mrs Tembey managed to get back to their home. They were afraid of looting, and the weather had broken so that rain was pouring in everywhere through the holes in the roof. Their fear of looting proved only too well founded. At No 30 the Powell family, whose house had been badly damaged, lost most of their valuables to a man who was happy to profit from other people's misfortunes.

But things were not so bad as they might have been. After the raid ended **MISS MOLLY POWELL** remembers climbing on to a tub to peer out of the manhole which was the emergency exit of the cellar shelter. At the same time her friend Nancie Webster looked out of the house next door in the dark of that December morning. She started to scream, and she screamed and screamed in horror. It took some time to convince her that the head and shoulders she had seen apparently lying on the ground were not really all that was left of Molly Powell, and that the rest of her was still all there below ground!

Miss Powell's father insisted that she should go to work so she struggled through the devastation to the LMS Railway headquarters on Granville Road. She passed the Abbeydale Picture House and saw the manager still in the evening dress he always wore, but now covered in dirt and blood. Her colleagues at work were aghast at her appearance, not having experienced any bombing in the areas where they lived.

Lastly here is the story of **MRS CONSTANCE DIXON** who was then Constance Bailey, living with her parents in Swaledale Road. She had taken First Aid and Auxiliary Nursing courses before the War broke out and she had been doing some work in a local hospital in her spare time. She writes:

On the evening of the first Sheffield Blitz I was at a Country and Scottish dancing class being held in the hall of the City Technical School at the corner of West Street and Leopold Street. During the dancing the caretaker came in to say that the air raid alarm had sounded, and we were advised to go into the school's air raid shelter. We went, but unfortunately the shelter smelled strongly of gas fumes to which I am allergic, so I decided to make for home and one of the men who lived in the same direction said he would accompany me.

As we made our way to Pinstone Street the sky was lit by a full moon and a glowing redness and we were met by the roar of planes overhead. We sprinted for a Nether Edge bus we saw coming past the Town Hall, but we had to swing on while the bus was in motion for the driver only slowed down momentarily as incendiary bombs were beginning to drop around us.

All the way to Nether Edge we seemed to be running through a wall of fire and at the terminus a passing Air Raid Warden directed us to a shelter under the shops (a shoe shop, if I remember rightly). Before we had settled down another warden came in to ask for any volunteers with a knowledge of first aid to come and help them. With the warden and our 'knowledge' to bolster us we had no idea as we set out of all we would have to face.

We made our way down Glen Road, passing the Tennis Club then being used as a barrage balloon site by the RAF, to the Abbeydale Council School. The wardens were using a small room near the entrance and there was a large shelter underneath occupied by many Abbeydale residents though some were in garden shelters. Some of these nearly became death traps when a landmine was dropped in Abbeydale Road close by. The force of the blast was terrifying, tearing up the side roads and lifting the sand bags covering garden shelters leaving them vulnerable to falling shrapnel.

One of the saddest moments of that particular episode was holding a wee baby who had a small piece of metal in its forehead and knowing there was no way we could get it to hospital for immediate treatment. Of course there were many other casualties, such as those rescued from houses on fire. The wardens worked like Trojans; nothing was too great a task for them and I saw them in the brilliant frosty moonlight fighting like supermen to put out fires on the roof of the school when it was hit by incendiary bombs. In my eyes none of them was particularly young. Some of them I knew personally: Mr Benson, Mr Butterworth who had often repaired my bike, and Mr Cantor who lived near my parents. No words of mine can fully encompass the admiration I felt for all the wardens on duty that night.

Around 6.00 am next morning I and Mr Cantor, who had had his spectacles blown from his face by the blast, made our way over Brincliffe Edge to our homes, not knowing what we should find. Some houses had received direct hits and many were damaged, but when I

The result of the bomb incident at Westbrook Bank viewed from the back garden of a house on Sharrow Vale Road.

saw my home I felt sure no one could have got out of it uninjured. I clambered in to look inside. There was nobody there. Everywhere there was dirt, dust, soot, broken glass, debris and there were machine gun bullets in the dining room furniture. The steel table-shelter looked undamaged but deserted.

I asked around among our neighbours but no-one knew where my parents were. Most people had taken refuge in a public shelter at the junction of Archer Lane and Montrose Road but this was an impossible trip for my mother who had for years suffered from rheumatoid arthritis (hence the table-shelter). As I found out later, when the crunch came she could not get into it and sat with my father in a small alcove leading to the dining room which certainly saved them from serious injury. I eventually traced them to my grandparents' house in Carterknowle Road which seemed unscathed. My mother was covered in soot from head to foot and my father's bald head was embedded with small pieces of glass. They were both terribly shocked but not so very surprised to see me. My father said that he felt all through that terrible night that I was safe, and he insisted that I should go to work as soon as I had seen to their comfort and had had a wash.

I set off for the City Centre. The detours were many and the scenes were tragic. Destruction and debris everywhere; buildings, buses and fire engines destroyed and burnt, holes in the roads, water mains burst, and worst of all the loss of life and the injured.

Of course I was very late for work. I was the last to arrive, and I was duly reprimanded by my boss for being so remiss! Most of the staff in the department lived to the north of the City or beyond and had just not realised the experience of those to the south and south west. Sadly they were brought face to face with it themselves two days later when the second Blitz of Sunday 15th December seemed to start where the other had left off, blasting from the Fargate end of the City and sweeping both north and eastwards, leaving death, injuries and destruction everywhere in its wake.

Strange how in a few weeks Sheffield seemed to be bustling again, though there were many blank areas until years later. I was invited to join the wardens at Abbeydale School and I still have my ARP badge, carefully polished, my armband which I embroidered myself in lax moments, a whistle and a folded black Appointment Card stating that Miss Constance Bailey was officially an Air Raid Warden from 1st January 1941.

With grateful thanks to all those who contributed their memories of the Blitz and made this account possible. It must inevitably leave out as much as it includes but we hope that it gives some idea of what local residents went through that night and of how much heroism and suffering must have gone unrecorded.

The day after the Blitz: bomb damage at Nether Edge Hospital.

OLD OAK AT BRINCLIFFE
NEAR SHEFFIELD

J.F.P JULY 30 1878

ACKNOWLEDGEMENTS

The names of those informants acknowledged in the articles have not been repeated here.

THE NEWBOULDS OF SHARROW BANK — The Archivist, Dorset County Library and the Regional Information Officer, Leamington Spa Library.

THE WILSONS AND THE SNUFF MILL — Information and permission to use material from his own book from Mr M H F Chaytor.

THE BOOT FAMILY — Mr I R Baines, grandson of Henry Boot and Mrs J Jenkinson, great granddaughter of William Boot of Heeley (born 1824).

THOMAS JESSOP — Staff at The Jessop Hospital for Women.

JOHN COLE OF PRIOR BANK — The Archivist, John Lewis Partnership.

THE NETHER EDGE BOWLING CLUB — Mr L R Gomersall who allowed access to the minutes of the Bowling Club.

OLD HOUSES AT THE TOP OF GLEN ROAD — Mr D Hewitt and Mrs M Kingsland.

THE BRINKCLIFFE TOWER ESTATE — Mrs F M Lavender, Robert Styring's granddaughter.

THE LANTERN THEATRE — Mr R Calnan, who was Chairman of the Dilys Guite Players, and Messrs Taylor and Emmett. Also staff at the Rudolf Steiner Life Centre, Tintagel House, and many local people who gave both information and kindness.
CHANGES AT SHARROW VALE — Mr and Mrs C Gilbert, Mrs F M Lavender and Mr A Mottram, the present owner of the former smithy.

TOM WHITTAKER — Personal memories of the late Mr T Whittaker noted in interviews.

LAURENCE MULLINS — Personal memories of the authors and from Mrs C Deacon, wife of Mr Mullins' grandson.

LESLIE PERKINS DE ABREW — Mrs M Abrew, widow, Mrs I Sharman, daughter, Dr M Flowerday, Mr R R Stapleton. Also Administrative Staff at Nether Edge Hospital, Mrs K Thompson, Miss S Anderson and Mr S Gallimore.

WILF GREEN — Personal information from Mr W Green himself.

Last, but not least, several of the authors are indebted to the staff of the Local History Library and the Sheffield Record Office for their unstinting help and we are deeply grateful to Elaine Nicholls for typing the copy.

ILLUSTRATIONS

We are indebted to the following people for allowing us to reproduce material in their possession:

Mrs M de Abrew, p. 60; Mr I R Baines, p. 27 (upper); Mr B Barstow, pp. 33 (lower), 34 (upper), 35, 61; Mr M H F Chaytor, pp. 12, 13, 14; Mrs C Deacon, p. 59; Mr C Gilbert, p. 57; Mr Wilf Green, pp. 62, 63; Miss Janet Hartley, pp. 47, 48, 49; The Jessop Hospital for Women, p. 32; Mrs F M Lavender, pp. 50, 51; Mrs R MacDonald, pp. 55 (lower), 56 (source unknown); Nether Edge Bowling Club, pp. 45, 46; Mr K Neville, pp. 64, 66, 68; Mr T H Pountney, pp. 21 (lower), 28 (lower); Mr G Robinson, pp. 4, 21 (autograph), 41, 55 (upper); Mr M Weston, pp. 9, 11 (lower), 16, 27 (lower), 36 (lower), 42 (upper right), 43; Mr T Whittaker, p, 58.

All other photographs are from Sheffield City Libraries and we are grateful to Mrs P. M. Coleman, Director of Information Services, for permission to reproduce them.

REFERENCES

THE ORIGINS OF NETHER EDGE AND SHARROW — Walton, Mary, *A History of the Parish of Sharrow Sheffield*, Sheffield, 1968. Together with material from the Fairbank Collection in the Sheffield Record Office and local newspapers, Ordnance Survey maps, sale plans, Burgess Rolls and Miscellaneous Documents in the Sheffield Local History Library.

ALEXANDER MACKENZIE — Addy, S. O., and Pike, W. T., *Sheffield at the Opening of the 20th Century: Contemporary Biographies*, Brighton [1900]; Hunter, Joseph, *Familiae minorum gentium*, ed. J. W. Clay, Harleian Society Publication, vols. 37–40, London, 1894–1896; Odom, W., *The History of St Paul's Church, Sheffield*, Sheffield, 1919, *Hallamshire Worthies*, Sheffield, 1926; Potts, J. D., 'Platts of Rotherham 1700–1810', Sheffield, 1959, *Local Pamphlets*, vol. 215 no. 12; Smith, M. S., 'The M'Kenzies of Finegand' (written 1889), *Local Pamphlets*, vol. 5 no. 9. Together with articles from various volumes of Newspaper Cuttings in the Sheffield Local History Library.

THE NEWBOULDS OF SHARROW BANK — *Census Returns*, Sheffield, 1851–1881; Goodfellow, A. W., 'Sheffield Turnpikes in the 18th Century', *Trans. Hunter Arch. Soc.*, vol. 5, Sheffield, 1943; Fairbank Collection; Hunter, Joseph, *Familiae minorum gentium*, ed. J. W. Clay, Harleian Society Publication, vols 37–40, London, 1894–1896; Local Directories; Miller, W. T., *Waterwheels of Sheffield*, Sheffield, 1936; *Newspaper Cuttings*, vols 8, 10, 27; Owen, F. M. 'Various Accounts, 1749', *Trans. Hunter Arch. Soc.*, vol. 5, Sheffield, 1937–43; Paulus, Carolus, *Manor and Parish of Ecclesall*, Sheffield, 1927; Sale Plans, Sharrow Bank 1881, Newbould Estate 1909; Sheffield Morning Telegraph – obituaries. The manuscripts examined in the Sheffield Record Office are too numerous to list. In addition, information was derived from documents in my own possession. J.F.

THE WILSONS AND THE SNUFF MILL — Chaytor, M. H. F., *The Wilsons of Sharrow*, Sheffield, 1962.

PUBLIC SERVICE AND PRIVATE PROFIT — Minutes of the Proceedings at Vestry Meetings of Ecclesall Bierlow (1808–1857); Sheffield and Rotherham Independent, June, July, 1844.

GEORGE WOSTENHOLM — Bexfield, H., *House of Wostenholm*, Sheffield, 1945; Coward, Henry, *Reminiscences of Henry Coward*, London, 1919; Hunter, Joseph, *Hallamshire*, ed. A. Gatty, Sheffield, 1869; Montgomery, James, *Memoirs of James Montgomery*, London, 1854; Odom, W., *Hallamshire Worthies*, Sheffield, 1926, *Memorials of Sheffield*, Sheffield, 1922; Sheffield Recreational Department, *History of the Botanical Gardens*, Sheffield, 1970; Stainton, J. H., *Making of Sheffield*, Sheffield, 1924; Tatton, Henry, *Old Sheffield Sketches and Notes*, Sheffield, 1920–36, MS in Sheffield Local History Library; Taylor, J., Editor, *Illustrated Guide to Sheffield*, Sheffield, 1879; Tweedale, G., 'George Wostenholm', *Giants of Sheffield Steel*, Sheffield, 1986; Walton, Mary, *A History of the Parish of Sharrow Sheffield*, Sheffield, 1968. Together with material from local directories, newspapers, census returns, maps, gravestones, sales plans, Miscellaneous Papers and Local Pamphlets in the Sheffield Local History Library and from the Bland Collection in the Sheffield Record Office.

JOHN RODGERS — Leader, R. E., *Sheffield Banking Company Limited*, Sheffield, 1916. Together with local directories, census returns, sale plans, newspapers and Ordnance Survey maps in the Sheffield Local History Library.

THOMAS STEADE — Stainton, J. B., *Making of Sheffield*, Sheffield, 1924; Walton, Mary, *A History of the Parish of Sharrow Sheffield*, Sheffield, 1968. Together with census returns, newspapers, directories, sale plans, Council Minutes, Ordnance Survey maps, Miscellaneous Papers in the Local History Library and the Parker Collection in the Sheffield Record Office.

JOHN BROWN AT SHIRLE HILL — *Illustrated London News*, November 21, London, 1863; Odom, W., *Hallamshire Worthies*, Sheffield, 1926; Schofield, M., 'The Genius of John Brown'. *Steel Times*, Sheffield, 1966; Tweedale, G., 'Sir John Brown (1816–1896)', *Greats of Sheffield Steel*, Sheffield, 1986. Together with articles from various volumes of Newspaper Cuttings in the Sheffield Local History Library.

THOMAS JESSOP — The Jessop Hospital for Women and various local directories and maps.

THE SMITHS — Himsworth, J. B.; 'Smith Edwin, and Theophilus His Son', *Trans. Hunter Arch. Soc.*, vol. 8, Sheffield, 1963; Odom, W., *Hallamshire Worthies*, Sheffield, 1926. Together with material from local directories, Ordnance Survey maps, graveyards, Council Minutes and Local Pamphlets in the Local History Library.

JAMES MONTGOMERY — From a pamphlet of unknown origin.

CHARLES PEACE — Ward, D., *The King of the Lags*, London, 1963.

JOHN COLE OF PRIOR BANK — *Chronicle for Cole Brothers*, vol. 15 no. 17, vol. 18 no. 20, 1961–1977; 'Deaf and Dumb Institute', *Endowed Charities*, London, 1897; *Men of the Period: England*, London, 1896; Prior Bank Sale Plan, 1913; Seed, T. A., *The History of the Norfolk Street Chapel*, Sheffield, 1907.

THEY BUILT NETHER EDGE — Odom, W., *Memorials of Sheffield*, Sheffield, 1922; *Sheffield and Rotherham 'Up to Date'*, London, 1897; Stainton, J. H., *Making of Sheffield*, Sheffield, 1924; Walton, Mary, *A History of the Parish of Sharrow Sheffield*, Sheffield, 1968. Together with material from the Fairbank Collection in the Sheffield Record Office, local directories, newspapers, Burgess Rolls, census returns, sale plans, Local Pamphlets, Miscellaneous Papers and Council Minutes in the Local History Library.

THE NETHER EDGE BOWLING CLUB — Pearson, John, *Stags and Serpents*, London, 1983.

THE LANTERN THEATRE — Seed, T. A., *The Sheffield Repertory Theatre*, Sheffield, 1959.

MEMORIES OF NETHER EDGE — Lamb, J. P., and Walton, Mary, *Raiders Over Sheffield*, Sheffield, 1980.